WILLIAMS
ON
PUBLIC DIPLOMACY

WILLIAMS
ON
PUBLIC DIPLOMACY

John Williams

IndieBooks

Williams on Public Diplomacy
by John Williams
Studies in Strategy and Communication I

ISBN: 978-1-908041-03-6
© 2012 John WIlliams

Published in 2012 by IndieBooks Limited
4 Staple Inn, London WC1V 7QH
IndieBooks.co.uk
ISBN: 978-1-908041-03-6
Printed by SRP, Bittern Road, Exeter EX2 7LW

To my wife, Pam

Contents

Preface

When countries were ruled by monarchs and emperors, diplomats could ignore the views of the masses and concentrate on influencing the ruler, their advisors. and the country's elite. But mass communication, mass literacy and the spread of democracy have changed this. Prime Ministers and Presidents have to listen to public opinion, including on international relations. Even dictators cannot entirely ignore the concerns of their citizens, for disapproval can be shown by protests and riots as well as at the polling station. So diplomacy now pays increasing attention to international public opinion, because the views of the public in other countries can not only help decide how that country behaves, but are also open to being influenced.

In the first half of the twentieth century, democracies and dictatorships developed the capability to influence public opinion in other countries through what they unblushingly called propaganda. In the second half, countries learned the hard way, in Suez and Vietnam, Algeria and Iraq, that domestic public opinion could not be taken for granted, and could itself be influenced from the outside.

In response to these trends, there has grown up an art or a science called 'public diplomacy': that is, international communication of all forms aimed not directly at foreign governments, but at their peoples. This is the subject-matter of this guide.

It is largely a practical art, with comparatively little academic study or mainstream analysis. Its practitioners rarely speak about how it works, what it can achieve – and its dangers. It is, after all, propaganda by another name, and while it can play a benign role in protecting national sovereignty or supporting human rights, it can also be used to deceive and repress. This makes it too important a subject to remain in the shadows.

It is also constantly changing: classic tools of public diplomacy, such as the BBC World Service or the Voice of America, are arguably less effective as the media land-scape fragments. Public diplomacy is becoming more about the creation of compelling narratives, the use of imagery and messages, the ability to respond quickly to events. In short, it uses the latest strategic communications techniques in an international setting.

Public diplomacy need not be any more immoral or dangerous than traditional diplomacy. How it is used is down to governments and through them to the people those governments represent. Its aims and uses should always be open to scrutiny. As well as a guide for prac-titioners and analysts, this book is also for the general reader, as a contribution to the cause of openness.

James Humphreys
Series Editor

Chapter One

Introduction

We are defined by words as well as by actions, by what we say as well as by what we do. Just as events are not always what they seem, so the way people see us is not always how we would like to be seen, our motives sometimes distressingly misunderstood, our good intentions misrepresented.

Governments, like people, need to explain and justify themselves if they are to be understood as they would like to be, and if they are to achieve the international aims they set themselves or find themselves having to grapple with. Countries can rarely afford to be indifferent to the way the world sees them, nor can they rely on their legitimate pursuit of self-interest going unchallenged by other countries. Perception can help or hinder the achievement of national goals. The way a country is seen can change with time or with a single traumatic or inspired event, and national reputation can differ widely from place to place, with inconvenient results if the nuances of global repute are not taken into account. Trade and tourism, diplomatic objectives and national self-esteem can all become hostage to the opinions of others.

This is a guide to public diplomacy as a form of international strategic communications: that is, how countries can advance their strategic objectives – or fail to – by the way they communicate with the world. It concentrates on political and diplomatic communication, rather than the branding of states or places, though a country is no more able to sell itself without regard to its reality than any other entity. In fact, perhaps less so, since countries tend to have histories from which there is no escape. But history is permanently revised by new facts and changing perspectives.

This guide is about examples, not theories. Take Britain: or is that England? Proud of our history, we are also prisoners of it. A recent Foreign Secretary, Jack Straw, used to say to his staff that wherever he went, Britain seemed obliged to help sort out problems left behind by empire. As his press secretary, I was with him as he dealt with crises and diplomatic problems relating to Kashmir, Gibraltar, Cyprus, Palestine, Afghanistan, Iraq and the United States of America. Britain – or is that the United Kingdom? – was unavoidably defined in all those places by that imperial legacy, as well as by current actions and interests. Sometimes there was inherited hostility, usually a measure of affection, sometimes an instinct to look to Britain for help.

When India and Pakistan were heading towards a possible nuclear war in 2002, they did not turn to Germany or Japan or Brazil – all larger countries – but to Britain, to shuttle discreetly between them and help find a way to avoid conflict. But a few years earlier, both countries had responded to an apparent British offer to mediate in the disputed province of Kashmir with a fury that would not have been shown to, say, Spain or Australia. The British government carries heavy baggage into every diplomatic waiting room. This can be to or against our benefit, depending on skill and luck in strategic communication and tactical handling. Our national goals, for the short and long term future, are complicated by the past, which has a way of intruding on the present.

More recently a different British government wrestled with decisions on intervention in Libya which were not confined to military considerations, but which involved strategic calculations about Britain's relations with the Arab world and about Britain's reputation – or not – as a country with some attachment to ideas of liberty. Britain's legitimate wish to engage with emerging Arab democracy could not be divorced either from the recent past of engagement with Colonel Gaddafi, nor erase all recollection of colonial occupation in the Middle East and Africa.

The leader of a former colony wishing to strengthen a weak position might choose to set himself against Britain: think of Robert Mugabe.

Then there is Europe, where Britain's current role is inescapably affected by a sense of history that is open to widely differing interpretation, obliging successive governments to struggle for a narrative that accommodates both reality and myth (in so far as they are distinguishable).

This is not an essay on British foreign policy, though that is where I have most professional experience of relevance to this series. Though there are passages about America, Israel, Palestine, Turkey, Tunisia, and Iran, it is inevitably Anglo-centric.

Rather than fixed rules, there are conclusions and general principles that emerge particularly from the real-world examples, and that offer readers some guidance on how to deal with their unique challenges. In fact, if there is one rule to be raised above all others it is to avoid thinking that one situation can be handled exactly like another, or even that the same problem can be handled precisely as it was last time. Strategy and communications and international relations all depend on context, which changes all the time.

Words and facts

In international relations, words can resonate over decades, or swiftly be made irrelevant. John Kennedy's speeches remain to some ears a reminder of a fine America, to others overblown rhetoric. This depends on your reading of history and your instinctive approach to politics. What cannot be denied is that Kennedy understood the power of beautifully crafted words to create room for action. When he supported the civil rights movement by telling southern segregationists their actions went against both the Bible and the US Constitution, he re-defined the argument decisively in favour of change (some would say belatedly) by conscripting two supreme sources of reference.

A leader's words can work powerfully to a country's advantage. Mikhail Gorbachev re-cast the Soviet Union's power relationships by popularising 'perestroika' and 'glasnost' as words that came to be associated with winding down tyranny. He could not have opened cordial and productive relationships with Ronald Reagan and Margaret Thatcher only by slogans, though – there had to be substance to his talk of reform and openness – but his strategic effort to end the Cold War on terms acceptable to Russia was given impetus by the communications strategy. Gorbachev was better able to achieve his ends with western leaders who believed, as did their electorates, that they were dealing not only with a charming individual but with a changing ideology. Words would not, before long, prevent the liquidation of the Soviet empire. But in that crucial period when the fall of the Soviet Union did not yet seem inevitable, Gorbachev created space in which to act on his own country's terms.

Perceptions and presentation

The lesson for communicators is that a country can change deeply-held perceptions even among enemies, crucially by changing behaviour, but also by symbolising change with words. Without skilled communications, Gorbachev might have been seen by Reagan as a weak young leader of a crumbling superpower (as Kennedy had been seen by Kruschev). But Reagan developed enough respect for the confident, non-confrontational agent of change in the Kremlin that he struck dramatic agreements in arms reduction that enabled Gorbachev to relieve his burden of military spending while appearing strong. He could not prevent history overtaking the Soviet Union, but history can be read only backwards. And as Gorbachev led his ailing country towards an uncertain future he extended his limited range of possibilities through superb self-presentation.

Reagan himself was a master of strategic self-presentation, whose rhetoric has served his historic reputation well. He is generously credited by many US commentators as the winner of the Cold War, partly because phrases like 'the evil empire' and 'tear down that Wall' seem in retrospect to have been the words of a man who knew which way history was going. Of course, he did not. Yet Reagan succeeded by floating high above the detail and projecting leadership through rhetoric. I remember a NATO meeting at which President Reagan gave a press conference of smiling generality, free of policy content or military detail, and left the stage to Secretary of State George Schulz to take questions on the mere facts. A phrase like 'It's morning in America' – of such powerful appeal to Americans wanting to move on from Vietnam and Watergate – is not open to fact-checking but matched exactly Reagan's image of folksy optimist.

However, for most communicators, facts are doggedly unavoidable, so it is essential to master at least the essential detail of the brief, and to ground strategy in some form of objective reality. It can be argued that Reagan's objective reality was not long in coming true, while Gorbachev's collapsed around him. But that is only one version of events that will always be open to interpretation. Similarly, President Obama's speech in Cairo soon after he took office appeared to transform Arab and Muslim views of America. Yet within months his and America's ratings were down again, and with them US leverage, as actions failed to match the rhetoric. For there must be some relationship between words and action for communication to be effective, though the way actions are perceived can be shaped by the words a country chooses.

What conclusions can be drawn from these examples? A national leader can use well-crafted words to make room for action, by changing perceptions of his or her country, by shaping others' understanding of the strategic situation, and thereby influencing partners' and opponents' own decisions. At its most skilled, this strategic use of communications technique can either achieve national goals, or prevent others imposing theirs. But there has to be some relationship between words and realities, even where facts are ambiguous and the course of events uncertain.

Public Diplomacy

What follows is a discussion of some outstanding instances of public diplomacy over the last 25 years, culminating in the Arab Spring. My experience has been first as a political journalist covering international events in the 1980s and 1990s, then as a British government spokesman in the period 1998-2006 which included the Kosovo conflict, 9/11 and the Iraq war, and most recently as an advisor to the Palestinian Authority. The judgements here are inevitably subjective, but one theme of this analysis is that subjectivity is what makes public diplomacy so important: few if any events can be seen in an 'objective' way that everyone would agree with. This is why countries need to take their public diplomacy seriously, if they wish to achieve their international objectives and protect their interests.

Technology

Public diplomacy is probably becoming more important and difficult in an age of more widespread and more rapid communications, which enable publics as well as decision-makers quickly to form subjectivejudgements that can have a major impact on the course of events. Texting is as crucial to modern revolutions as barricades once were. The modern dictator is much less able to control either his own public opinion or international perception when smartphones and laptops are showing brutal images instantly. And a modern democrat must contend with proliferating forms of individual communication, such as political bloggers, which operate outside familiar institutional frameworks and power relationships. The international financial markets, with their instant communications and momentary judgements based on sentiment as well as economics, now break governments more quickly than newspapers or parliaments. It is doubtful that Italy's parliament would have ousted Silvio Berlusconi but for a loss of international market confidence caused by the way the country was perceived and which led to unsustainable interest rates being levied on Italian government debt.

Precedents

However, it is always worth keeping some historical perspective and reminding ourselves that public diplomacy is not entirely modern. After the defeat of France in 1940, Charles De Gaulle had little more than words and symbols to sustain France's independence – one reason he was so touchy about his own status and so concerned to acquire the means to broadcast to the French people himself. Though marginalised by Roosevelt and Churchill, he epitomised 'a certain idea of France' and built a movement that began to return to France its dignity and confidence. Churchill's eloquence was not only a national inspiration in 1940, but influenced an isolationist United States into providing crucial support to Britain before its own entry into the war. President Franklyn Roosevelt projected an idea of a benign and strong America a generation before Kennedy and a lifetime before Obama, while taking care not to be photographed in his wheelchair (in an age when the media subjected itself to a level of self-censorship unimaginable today). These great democratic figures of the mid-20th century understood the power of words and images to project their countries, as did Stalin: for much of his lifetime, the Soviet Union managed to conceal the reality of Stalinism behind a revolutionary image that had a tenacious in many democracies. The image was powerful enough to drown the voices of those like the writer George Orwell who saw through to the brutal reality of 'Uncle Joe's' regime; and even blind those who visited Russia to see for themselves in the 1930s and returned as Stalin's supporters or apologists.

So the projection of a country's self-image can have malign uses, and on a lower scale of wrongness, public diplomacy is self-evidently open to abuse by distortion, cynicism or selective versions of disputable facts. But in many, perhaps most, circumstances, it is entirely legitimate for a country and its leaders to portray ambiguous events and complex situations in ways that strengthen their international standing or their negotiating hand.

Throughout this book, case studies will be used to illustrate the uses and abuses of public diplomacy, and some conclusions will be offered at the end of each chapter, with some overall conclusions and reflections in the final. The aim is to offer practical suggestions, through real examples, for those engaged in public diplomacy and international strategic communications, while giving the general reader an insight into this powerful and little-known art.

Chapter Two

Principles

In using public diplomacy to pursue strategic objectives, there are some general principles which can be drawn from the case studies here. The cases are not chosen to illustrate principles, but rather, the principles arise from studying practical examples. The reason for this is that the trade, profession, or craft which is analysed here is not a theoretical or academic discipline which can be practised effectively by reference to fixed principles imposed on situations. The practitioner has to decide afresh, every time, what the problem or opportunity is, what can be applied to it from experience and what must be improvised by a combination of intuitive thinking and tried technique. The working principles exist only in practice, not in a rulebook.

Reality matters

The first general principle is that strategic communications must be grounded in reality – that is, a recognisably accurate version of events that carries conviction internationally. This principle is vividly illustrated by the rise and fall of President Obama's standing in the Middle East, after early expectations led to disappointment in the region. His policy was broadly welcomed there when he announced it; but as the perceived gap between rhetoric and reality widened, the US position carried less conviction.

Why not put this first principle more simply, that governments must tell the truth about reality? The trouble is that 'reality' is not a solid or immovable object whose nature is unarguably obvious to all: events are ambiguous and complex, capable of bearing more than one interpretation by reasonable people who have different perspectives, interests or values. There is also a role for advocacy in setting out a position in such a way as to convince others and build support for it. Indeed, advocacy is a crucial element of leadership, though it can of course be misused. Churchill's wartime speeches are often cited as powerful examples of leadership; they did not seek to set out 'both sides' of the conflict, even though at other times Churchill would recognise that Germany had some legitimate grievances with the Treaty of Versailles. So the second general principle is that the way events and consequences are seen is shaped by the way they are described, not determined by some unarguable 'reality'. A country which succeeds in defining a situation on its own terms can widen its scope for action while limiting that of others. To see events as shaped by argument it is not necessarily a cynical approach. Indeed, countries with benign objectives like the strengthening of human rights need to be as robust and skilled as those who would defend harsh actions by necessity or use self-serving arguments for setting freedoms aside.

A country is entitled to advance its narrative by clear explanation, giving a sense of legitimate national purpose, with the important proviso of respecting principle number one, that its narrative is recognisably accurate. It is a delusion that there can be one 'objective' way of describing a situation that looks very different to the participants. It is more honest to accept this than to accuse one party or other of lying or misleading, or to claim your own version as the only truth. This principle is closely examined in the case study on Israeli and Palestinian public diplomacy, a classic example of a situation in which 'reality' very much depends on point of historical, religious or cultural view.

However, if a national narrative begins to deviate from a description which most observers would regard as reasonable, then it pays a price in legitimacy. This can happen where a country is making a case in language which may appeal to one of its audiences across the world, while antagonising others. So a third general principle is that successful public diplomacy needs to understand its audiences. An example of this problem was the Bush administration's use of the terms 'Crusade' and 'War on Terror', which gathered a good deal of domestic and European support after the attack on the World Trade Centre in New York on 11 September 2001, while reducing support among many Muslims, who felt that this term bracketed their faith with terrorism.

know and think – their awareness, understanding or attitudes, and even the intensity with which they hold their views or opinions and the extent to which their positions are open to change. Of course, shaping knowledge or attitudes is not an end in itself: governments and others may still act in ways that run counter to public opinion. But it is a way of seeing if public diplomacy is having an impact and exploring the environment in which decision-makers are working.

Chapter Three

The Arab Spring

The phrase 'Arab Spring' is an example of how complex events can come to be understood, or misunderstood, through a description that dominates commentary. It brackets a series of events in diverse countries, with local origins and varying consequences, using two assumptions. The first is that they have a common theme and the second is that the theme is optimistic. There was an alternative description available as these events broke out, which was not optimistic at all. This was that the stability of the Middle East was under threat as responsible rulers were besieged by mobs who would replace them not with democracy, but anarchy, in which Islamic fundamentalists would prosper. Either interpretation was likely to be a caricature.

This book is not intended to make historical judgements, but to look at the way events are seen, and to an extent shaped, by the words that describe them. 'Arab Spring' expressed a belief or hope that these events from Tunisia to the Arabian Gulf were a benign development: the first interpretation rather than the second.

The phrase is obviously not a case of planned public diplomacy to achieve a chosen end. Rather, it gives an insight into the way that media and politicians grope for a narrative lifeline amid the fog of events. Once a phrase is taken hold of, everyone continues to use it as a kind of guide. 'Arab Spring' offered itself as a way of understanding the revolts in Tunisia, Egypt, Libya, Syria, Yemen and Bahrain as a Middle Eastern version of the 'Prague Spring' of 1968, in which Czechs rose up against the Soviet Union. By using this loose, implicit analogy, leaders and commentators (and often the rebels themselves) were emphasising the hopeful characteristics of the Arab uprisings – against dictatorship, towards freedom – while making reference to their fragility, since the Czech uprising failed.

The first country to overthrow a dictator, Tunisia, produced a leader who grasped the importance of public diplomacy in enhancing his own, his party's and his country's reputation. Rachid Ghannouchi, leader of the Ennahda party, presented himself skilfully as an Islamist who believed in sharing power with secular democrats. Ghannouchi, who had been long exiled in England, understood the need to reassure international opinion, not least as Tunisia's tourism and trade had been badly affected by loss of confidence in the country's stability. This presented an incoming government with a formidable challenge. One of the main causes of the revolution had been high youth unemployment, so it was essential to re-build Tunisia's income quickly through improved international confidence. Ghannouchi, as a political thinker with admirers across the Arab world, was conscious too of his responsibility as the vanguard of what was seen as a regional revolution. That responsibility was to show that Islamic parties need be neither anti-democratic nor violent. Female candidates were given prominence to counter fears that women would suffer from an Islamic victory. Although this was done mainly to reassure Tunisian voters, interviews were given as well to international media, with the image of the country and of the region in mind.

Having won most seats, but not a majority, Ghannouchi's party kept its word by forming a coalition with secular rivals, establishing a potential model for Muslim democracy. Ghannouchi seemed to be genuine in his effort to forge a democratic version of Islamism, though his party's conduct over a long period would be the proof, rather than well-chosen words. The words – the commitment – gave Tunisia the room in which to cultivate its young democracy if it could.

Meanwhile in Egypt, whose size made it a more important model whichever way it went, the balance between democracy and Islam was far more uncertain. The military added a menacing element to the mix, undoing the strong impression that their refusal to fire on the protestors had made at the start of the revolution. In Syria, President Assad and his family responded immediately to unrest by unleashing the Army, and as the bloodshed continued it was no longer possible to see the regional convulsion as a series of essentially peaceful uprisings, as in Tunisia. But 'Arab Spring' continued to be the label. Despite the autumn of bloodshed in Egypt, the brutal tactics of the Syrian regime throughout the year, and the civil war in Libya, the broadly positive view of the Arab Spring persisted in the Middle East. The University of Maryland's annual survey of Arab public opinion in October 2011 had 55% saying they were optimistic about the future of the Arab world, 16% pessimistic, while large majorities expressed support for the rebellions.

The most striking example of a country using the 'Arab Spring' to strengthen its position by public diplomacy was Turkey: not an Arab country, but a secular democracy with a Muslim majority population, and a leadership which saw an opening to make strategic gains as a regional power. Prime Minister Erdogan made a series of interventions which, in the words of *Foreign Policy* magazine, 'achieved a level of influence in the Middle East it [Turkey] hasn't had since the collapse of the Ottoman Empire'.

The Turkish PM was voted *Time* magazine's Person of the Year. Turkey was seen in the Annual Survey of Arab Opinion mentioned above as the country which had played the most constructive role, Prime Minister Erdogan was the most admired regional leader in the five countries polled, and 44% of Egyptians wanted their country to look like Turkey, with France second on ten per cent and

Saudi Arabia third on 8%. Iran rated under one per cent. Turkey's competition with Iran to strengthen their relative influence as Muslim – but not Arab – powers in the region was a strategic subplot in the tussle of public diplomacy.

One interesting insight from this five-country poll was an improvement in approval of the United States, from 10% in 2010 to 26% in 2011. Professor Shibley Telhami, who oversaw the survey, offered this explanation: 'This improvement could be related to the perception of the American handling of the Arab Spring, as 24% of those polled identified the US as one of the two countries they believe played the most constructive role in the Arab Spring.' In contrast, Turkey was number one, on 50%.

Like Turkey, Qatar saw an opportunity in the Arab Spring to assert itself. The small but wealthy Gulf state was early to support the uprisings in Egypt, Libya and Syria, despite its own lack of democracy. The common thread was championing Sunni Islamists, in what a *Financial Times* editorial of 1 December 2011 described as a 'pragmatic' policy of strengthening itself with movements likely to have increasing influence throughout the Arab world'.

Qatar is host to one of the most powerful instruments of public diplomacy in the Arab world, the Al Jazeera television channel, which is by far the most watched outlet in the region. Its decisions on how to report events can influence the events themselves. *Foreign Policy* magazine described its role in reporting the Arab Spring as 'a revolutionary inspiration in its own right'. Any public diplomacy effort in the Arab world has to achieve prominence on Al Jazeera if it is to have any chance of making an impact.

With the events of the 'Arab Spring' still unfolding unpredictably, it would be risky to draw conclusions that are too firm about its direction and impact. But Turkey's high standing shows how a country can assert its role through public diplomacy without taking any actions in substance. Prime Minister Erdogan made his interventions not by negotiating treaties but essentially by a well-timed visit to make a major speech to the Arab League, while distancing Turkey from Israel (there is further discussion of this in a chapter on Israel).

On the strategically important issue of Islamism and democracy, the only way that this can be judged is whether countries like Tunisia, Egypt and Morocco (where there was no revolution, but an Islamist party won an election while presenting itself as modelled on Turkey) actually emerge with Islamist parties in government, respecting democracy. But Rachid Ghannouchi's performance in Tunisia had already underlined an important point, that movements for change need personalities who symbolise their direction, as he sought to do – and as Prime Minister Erdogan did in Turkey. The Turkish leader was not only projecting an idea of his country, but an idea of Muslim democracy governed by an explicitly Islamist party in a secular society.

Chapter Four

Europe and the United Kingdom

For a British spokesman, the European Union presents special challenges. UK membership is a permanently live political issue on which our robust media has aggressive views and, in some cases, a sense of mission about shaping rather than reporting the politics. The issues in the media are often tediously complicated, while touching raw political nerves. The process of resolving them can be laborious and procedurally obscure. And the whole enterprise is inherently ambiguous in relation to nationhood and sovereignty.

Handling EU policy in the media is a case study in striking the balance between detail and simplicity. The detail is open to media exploitation: political correspondents – known as 'the lobby' at Westminster – are skilled at seizing on a point of detail and using it to skew public understanding. This is not dishonest, but neither is an exercise in rational discussion of policy options or of the national interest; never mind of elucidating the choices and trade-offs that a nation makes within this union of sovereign democracies.

However, if government allows itself to become too focused on narrow arguments about apparently arcane matters, it loses the chance to make the strategic case, while inadvertently strengthening public and media perception of the EU as a permanent exercise in being out of touch. Take as an example the issue of qualified majority voting, or QMV. The first problem is that even in discussing such matters, it is necessary to slip into using off-putting jargon. QMV was one of the issues under discussion at an important European Council held in Nice in 2000. The European Council is the regular meeting of heads of government and foreign ministers. This is an unwieldy decision-making process which, for all its faults, belies the caricature of the EU as a Brussels bureaucracy by putting the big questions on the table before elected Prime Ministers, who make collective choices by a combination of skill, bluff and exhaustion.

The Nice meeting had before it a series of reforms designed to adapt the Union to the arrival of new members from Eastern Europe. For Britain, this was a moment of achievement for a long-standing objective, known by the unappealing word 'enlargement': in fact, the exciting goal of re-uniting Europe across the East-West divide of the Cold War. Here surely was something to admire, even celebrate, as an unmistakably historic event, which Britain had championed. Yet as the Nice summit approached, it was clear that the British media would narrow the focus of this event to difficult issues like QMV, difficult both in the challenge of explaining them and in their potential for being portrayed as threats to the national interest.

The point about EU voting is that it needs to reflect the varying sizes of the countries around the table. If Germany, France and Italy could be outvoted by Malta, Luxembourg, Latvia and Estonia, this would be undemocratic in terms of the populations involved. So in the Council, ministers do not vote by a simple majority on a show of hands. Instead, the majority is qualified to take account of each country's population: hence the term Qualified Majority Voting. Few people can be expected to know of or be interested in this, and even fewer to know the formula by which the weighting is done (for QMV did not work simply by totting up populations, otherwise a few big countries could too easily dominate).

The communications challenge at Nice was that in deciding on the voting weights of the new members, the EU would also need to make decisions about the voting weights of existing members, within the expanded Council. Inevitably the established countries like Britain would find themselves with comparatively less weight, within a bigger union. While this was mathematically obvious, it was politically dangerous. Britain's eurosceptic media – eurosceptic also being a term of jargon – saw this reform as a chance to portray Europe as diminishing British sovereignty by weakening our voting strength. Note that words like 'weak' and strong' can be used very easily to shape – or distort – public understanding of complexity.

This reform of voting weights was not the only problem. While making this change, it was proposed that some categories of decision would become subject to QMV and no longer subject to individual country veto. The word 'veto' was, like 'weak' and 'strong', an easy signal for the media to use to readers, especially when attached to the word 'surrender', as in surrendering the British veto. Note how appealing these words are by comparison with EU jargon. Championing 'enlargement' struggled to compete with the charge of 'surrendering the veto'.

How to deal with this, without surrendering to the eurosceptic media? This mattered. It was not a game. The British government at the time believed profoundly that Britain would be stronger – that word – as a major influence in an enlarged Union. Indeed, as many of the new members from the East shared the British approach on many issues, it was likely that the UK would wield more influence in the enlarged Union, especially if it worked constructively, and not with reluctance, to design the mechanics. But this did not seem likely to be the way the Nice summit was going to be reported and perceived, and so there was a danger that this British objective would lack public confidence.

It could not be assumed that the historic significance of re-uniting Europe would automatically outweigh the tactical objections of media opponents. There was drama in the detailed battle, and in the scope for government failure: the administration of the preceding Prime Minister, John Major, had been racked by divisions on Europe and by hostile media coverage. Events in Europe would once again play back into domestic politics. Failure is always a story, and a more readily packaged one than some enormous strategic development on so broad a canvas as to be hard to focus the public's immediate attention. The British government needed to work to keep the strategic panorama in view, while closing down the scope for being judged to have failed on points of detail.

Three tactical decisions were taken. One, was to engage heavily on the detail with political correspondents well in advance of the summit, despite what some officials saw as the certainty that 'the lobby' would distort the reality whatever effort was made, so it would be better to offer them as little to distort as possible. This reluctance was understandable, given many years of officials and ministers feeling they had attended a different summit and negotiated a different agreement to the one they read about in the newspapers. But it was judged better to take the risk of engaging and arguing over an extended period.

The second decision was to set the negotiations within a robust framework that reminded the public of the long-term British interest in getting the detail right. The objective was described as 'a stronger Britain in a wider Europe'. The government took head-on the eurosceptic narrative by insisting that this process would make Britain stronger. It would do so because 'a wider Europe' would be stronger in the world, and Britain was going to play an active role within it. 'Wider Europe' was chosen as a more appealing way of describing the unification of East and West than the humdrum 'enlargement'.

This easily-spoken, non-jargon phrase, a stronger Britain in a wider Europe, was a reasonable description of the facts: contestable, open to democratic dispute, but not a distortion nor an exaggeration, and measurable by reference to the detailed reforms (provided Britain could achieve its negotiating aims on the detail).

The third tactical decision was for the Foreign Secretary, Robin Cook, to give the media a set of eight benchmarks a month ahead of the summit by which to judge the outcome. This made the point: 'we are going to deal on the facts, openly, and we are going to carry this argument to the public, asking for a fair-minded judgement.' There was a psychological element to this. Government could not go on backing away from arguments about Europe for fear of the media. It was time for some confidence. The media responded well. One long-serving political correspondent observed that the government was 'trusting us with the facts'. The result was an argument about the facts, not about a sideshow created by the media, an enormous gain.

Once engaged, the argument had to be won. It was no good accepting the media assumption that any extension of QMV would necessarily weaken Britain. A small number of examples were chosen to illustrate bad policies which Britain had been unable to change because others used their veto against us. The point was that the veto needed to be preserved for truly major decisions, so that the much-derided 'Brussels bureaucracy' could not choke decision-making where action was in our own interest. This argument needed to be made with care so that the issues at Nice were not reduced to us-against-them. The zero-sum assumption needed to be challenged, so that a foothold could be gained for the novel idea that everyone might gain from sensible reform that made a wider Europe effective and representative.

The British strategy was to underline the value of a balance between national and collective interest. This was encapsulated in the most important benchmark, that the new minimum vote necessary for a blocking minority within QMV would not fall below a certain population level (which gave a modest additional protection to the UK and other larger states). In other words, while working co-operatively within the new system, Britain would be sure of defending its interests by joining with like-minded allies.

That benchmark was achieved in the negotiation – though only just – and when Robin Cook presented his original set of benchmarks at the concluding press conference, the media verdict was that they had overall been delivered. That is not to say that the eurosceptic media declared Nice a triumph, of course. But this difficult and complex negotiation had been reported in a way that gave some visibility to Britain's objectives and thus enabled the public to make a judgement, while grasping the wider strategic interests at stake.

A government spokesman should not ask for more than that the actual policy is open to challenge and debate, grounded in a version of facts and events that is not unreal. This is the least the public deserves in a democracy: that in the fog of dispute over policy and actions, something real is discernible by which to judge elected representatives on their motives and delivery.

Five years later, the European Union ran into difficulty over a more ambitious reform programme, the attempt to agree an EU constitution. This was from the start a difficult challenge for the British government, since much of media and Parliament saw this as an exercise in expanding EU powers at the expense of national sovereignty. The British government had little appetite for negotiating a European constitution, either in principle or as a practical matter, as it would present formidable problems in Parliament. But once the project developed irresistible momentum among Heads of Government at the European Council, tactical decisions were necessary on two fronts: one, to limit the scope of treaty changes and two, to neutralise domestic opposition. These two objectives were obviously linked. The government judged that it could carry reform through if it defined limited objectives in a way that secured a critical level of support while preventing opponents establishing a veto through the media. The strategic context for these tactical considerations was the judgement that Britain must remain positively engaged in European decision-making, and not allow the EU to become a series of defensive actions leading to increasing isolation, and accompanied by media scorn that undermined public approval of the whole EU enterprise. Rightly or wrongly, the Blair government felt this had been the strategic mistake of the previous government under John Major.

So the tactical decision was taken to speak positively about selected elements of the proposed constitution, in order to show that the reform could strengthen the sovereignty of nations within the context of an effective union. Ministers pre-empted media criticism of, for example, the proposal to create a role of President of the Council, arguing that this figure, chosen by national prime ministers to chair their meetings, could be a counter-weight to the centralising tendency of the European Commission in Brussels. The wider argument was made that this reform fitted the British idea of the EU as a balance between the collective strength of Europe and the national sovereignty of its countries. The phrase used was a 'union of nations', in an attempt to summarise the complex and ambiguous arrangement by which many nation states seek to strengthen themselves by pooling some of their sovereignty.

This effort did not succeed in turning the tide of media opinion in Britain, which had for many years been running against the EU. Arguably it enabled Britain to take a constructive negotiating position in framing the constitution, rather than be forced one by one into reluctant concessions. The proposal to create a so-called European 'foreign minister' (that is, a representative of the 27 ministers on the Foreign Affairs Council) was in practice limited through negotiation to operating only where the nations chose to have a joint policy; not where they exercised the sovereign right to have their own approach to a foreign policy issue. This was an important limitation, though in media terms the 'European foreign minister' tag was impossible to counter as evidence of centralised EU power.

The power of the eurosceptic media was demonstrated by *The Sun* and *The Daily Mail* opening a campaign on the same day for a referendum on the constitution. These newspapers, rather than parliamentary Opposition, set the agenda by making a demand which it was difficult for democratic politicians to resist. This was done with a vigour and directness which political campaigners rarely match. The Foreign Secretary, Jack Straw, became so concerned about negative attitudes which he encountered while canvassing in local elections that he persuaded the Prime Minister to promise a referendum in the next Parliament.

Meanwhile other countries were conducting referenda while the legislation approving the EU constitution was going through the House of Commons. The French referendum became critical when opinion polls there turned unexpectedly from Yes to No.

It was clear by the evening of the French referendum that Britain was going to be in a very difficult position if the result was No. It would be impossible to continue with parliamentary ratification; yet to withdraw the legislation would bring on to Britain the blame for killing the constitution, at a time when French ministers were insisting they would try again. As well as the issue of blame, there was the rightness and wrongness of persisting with legislation in a way that seemed to be part of a wider effort by European governments to ignore public opinion. This would be especially dangerous politically in eurosceptic Britain.

The decision of substance was clear: Britain needed to suspend its legislation. But this needed to be done in a way which kept the problem focused where it should be, on those governments which had lost referenda, not on the British government which had all along been lukewarm about the constitution.

The desired outcome was achieved by a simple phrase, agreed by the Prime Minister and Foreign Secretary, and used by Jack Straw in a press conference the moment the French result was announced. There needed, he said, to be a 'period of reflection'. This avoided the course being urged on Britain by the French government, to say immediately that it would continue with its own parliamentary process; while avoiding the opposite trap, of being seen to give the constitution its coup de grace. There was no need to be more specific, as the media understood the significance. Britain was taking heed of Europe-wide public concerns, but doing so unaggressively, in a way that left options open for later. This tactical decision was as much about the way it was communicated – deftly, decisively – as about any diplomatic manoeuvres behind the scenes. In fact, the French government had to accept the position once the Foreign Secretary told his counterpart that he was going to be calling for a period of reflection – France understood the impact that this phrase would have. And by doing this promptly in public, the government dealt with domestic opponents, who could not reasonably ask for more.

By the time Parliament reconvened a few days later, it was so taken for granted that the legislation would be suspended that it was done without controversy. The EU constitution remained suspended until new leaderships across Europe re-introduced the reforms as the Lisbon Treaty.

This is not an example of a country using public diplomacy to achieve strategic aims or advance its interests, but rather to avoid even worse difficulties while preserving a major strategic interest: in this case, positive engagement in the European Union against a background of public unease and media hostility.

Among the conclusions that can be drawn are some

points about language as a tactical instrument. It is necessary to strike the right balance between detail and simplicity, when explaining complex international issues, especially in the face of a hostile media. Simple words can be used by skilled opponents to distort subtle or complex issues, so it is tactically wise to choose similarly plain language for your own case. Avoid jargon, or risk losing the initiative to opponents who speak more clearly. These are good points for any communicator; but they have their own value in international relations, where there is a tendency to slip into the clichés of diplomacy, for governments to talk among themselves and lose the audience on which consent rests. It is a peculiarity of diplomacy that for many of those practising it, there is greater comfort in the technical jargon with its references to all the relevant texts and treaties, than there is in unbundling the complexity with plain language. It may arise from a mix of the pride of the insider, who has mastered the specialist terms, and also the temptation to avoid clear language as a way of covering up a lack of thought or unwelcome realities. Whatever the cause, it is a useful rule to talk and write to one another in meetings and options papers in language the public would understand. This can help overcome the tendency to show familiarity with the subject by gliding over the acronyms without thinking in any depth. Ministers themselves are seduced by this private language, since they are almost always non-experts struggling to impose themselves upon the experts. This is not a trivial point: it is harder to question assumptions and to challenge orthodoxies without the nerve to say: 'what does this actually mean? What impact will it have in the real world?' This has obvious importance in unearthing the strategic points among the clutter of detail in European Union business.

The main tactical conclusion of this case study is that setting public benchmarks ahead of difficult events is often a risk worth taking, for the sake of showing confidence, giving the public clarity and challenging the media to measure events on your own terms rather than theirs. Do not assume that obvious strategic gains (to government) will be obvious to an indifferent public who have many other things to worry about, getting its limited information from media with their own preoccupations and prejudices. Nor is it safe to assume that strategic gains will necessarily outweigh the arguments over detail. The stakes have to be set out clearly, with signposts to the higher ground.

As in the last chapter, there is an illustration here, in the EU constitution episode, of the way words can be as important as actions. A public intervention can be used to deal decisively with a complex diplomatic problem, by making clear internationally and domestically what option will be taken, and doing so sufficiently clearly that there is no question of a subsequent change of mind and no purpose in bringing diplomatic pressure to bear from outside. This can be more effective than trying to reach agreement behind the scenes, if a government decides the circumstances are right: for example, that it must break free from a trap.

Further, reviewing several episodes in recent EU history underlines the value of resilience. For the British government, at least, there is unlikely to be much credit or understanding for its positions, or sympathy for its dilemmas, either from its own public or from international partners. But the temptation to shut down in public should be resisted. While short silences – refusing some interviews, saying little on the doorstep – can be a tactical device, countries have to make themselves heard above the noise. Never give up on battles that seem hopeless causes, or give in to relentless media pressure. The only route to salvation is to engage.

Chapter Five

Kashmir

When countries misread each others' intentions, the consequence can be war. In 2002, India and Pakistan misread one another's intentions over Kashmir, bringing two states armed with nuclear weapons closer to conflict than either realised. While neither mistook the other's seriousness, there was a dangerous mismatch on both sides between reality and perception over each other's thresholds. The scene was set for catastrophe, as was clear to the British government from the well-informed reporting of its diplomats in the two capitals.

India believed that Pakistan would not use its nuclear weapons because India's superior power would make this suicidal. Pakistan believed India would not use its nuclear weapons overwhelmingly, precisely because India had the capacity to wipe Pakistan out: unthinkable. Since India would not dare use its overwhelming power in full, Pakistan believed any exchange would be confined to 'tactical' strikes, that is, attacks which obliterated a major city or two on each side. The world would intervene before this went beyond control, forcing terms on India. Against this rash assumption, India felt secure (just as rashly) against any form of nuclear attack because of its preparedness to destroy its neighbour. India massed huge conventional – non-nuclear – forces at the border opposite Lahore, ready to take the city if Pakistan refused to cease attacks across the border hundreds of miles away in Kashmir: Lahore would then be a kind of hostage. India was convinced Pakistan would not trigger nuclear war over Lahore. Pakistan meanwhile was determined that if India moved those forces on Lahore, then Pakistan would launch a nuclear retaliation. So Lahore was Pakistan's nuclear threshold: not realising this, India was preparing to attack it.

This presented Britain with challenges in public diplomacy with unusually high stakes. The first question was whether to raise a global alarm about the seriousness of the risk of nuclear conflict, or to make a low-key effort to encourage two nuclear powers to move backwards without loss of face. The Foreign Secretary, Jack Straw, decided on a low-key approach, as he spoke in turn to the two national leaderships, judging that their mutual trading of aggressive rhetoric needed to be ended so that discreet steps away from conflict could be taken. In other words, the public diplomacy strategies of each country were – between them – a major factor in making war increasingly likely. Leaders were kicking away their ladders of retreat. So if either did decide to back down, it might by then have become politically impossible.

But the quiet approach presented a dilemma. Britain

had a serious duty of care for its own citizens in India and Pakistan, as well as to British citizens of Indian and Pakistani origin with families in the sub-continent, and more generally to the many millions likely to be affected as fall-out drifted across the sub-continent and the region's health and other public services collapsed with catastrophic consequences way beyond the immediate – enormous – casualties. There would need to come a point at which the British government was obliged to issue a grave warning. But at that point any leverage would probably be lost, and so to warn people of impending nuclear war might itself hasten that war. Such an announcement would be likely to cause panic once people grasped the imminence of conflict, but to delay beyond a certain point would result in even worse panic, and chaos on roads, railways and at airports. It was clear to Britain that the timetables on which the two sides were working already presented severe logistical challenges for the airlines if these huge countries were to be evacuated.

After several days of shuttle diplomacy, it was decided that there could be no further delay, and that the duty of care had come to override the challenge of diplomacy – the process of evacuation must begin, with a solemn warning issued by the Foreign Secretary to British nationals. In fact, when this moment arrived, this turned out unexpectedly to be the action which prevented war.

India protested that warning British citizens to leave would have a terrible impact on India's economy. The

Foreign Secretary pointed out that war between nuclear powers would have an even greater economic impact. This made India realise – as diplomacy hadn't – that the strategy of confrontation backed by a nuclear threat was in danger of becoming a bluff that Pakistan called, catastrophically for both. India began taking the sort of de-escalatory steps that until this point Britain had been unable to persuade either side to agree to, and Pakistan took steps backward in its turn.

There was no war. The deterrent turned out to be a media appearance by the British Foreign Secretary in his Blackburn constituency, which was finally enough to make the potential combatants realise how close they were to mutual destruction.

The diplomacy which helped to avoid this conflict between nuclear states was so discreet that few ever realised how serious the threat of war had become. There is no right or wrong about quiet diplomacy or high profile intervention – tactical judgements must be made about the right mix at the right moments. It may be that India and Pakistan might have been deterred by strident calls for de-escalation and an atmosphere of international alarm expressed with great urgency. This cannot now be known. All that can be said is that the judgement to give both countries the room in which to manoeuvre themselves away from the brink was vindicated, though the catalyst was perhaps unintended.

Quiet diplomacy is sometimes the best way, but

it carries obvious risks. Though it worked over Kashmir in 2002, there would have been severe criticism of the British government had war broken out before the scale of the likely conflict had been made clear. It would have been no use saying that a great deal of quiet diplomacy had gone on, had many lives been lost. On a lesser scale – because no nuclear weapons were involved – Britain faced repeated criticism for using quiet diplomacy in dealing with Zimbabwe in a series of crises from 1999 onwards, the year in which President Robert Mugabe began to use land confiscation as a political weapon. Whenever a British minister, for example Peter Hain, made criticisms, the Zimbabwean President turned to his advantage the impression of the old colonial power telling an independent African state what to do. When Britain instead worked quietly to encourage African neighbours to apply pressures which the Zimbabwean leader would find it harder to ignore, the UK was condemned for weakness. In fact, there was a moment in September 2001 when Britain worked with Nigeria and a small number of like-minded Commonwealth countries, including Barbados, to convene a conference at which their pressure – not Britain's – produced a satisfactory agreement. It was never tested because within a few days international attention swung away from Southern Africa, following the attack on New York's Twin Towers.

Chapter Six

Public Diplomacy in Wartime

Wars are self-evidently determined by events on the ground. More than any situation in international relations, there is a brute force about events in a conflict that cannot be ignored or explained away. And yet there is often an important role for international communications during war. The most obvious is that a country needs to explain and justify its reasons for war. Another is that it must protect and advance its interests in any diplomacy surrounding the conflict.

There is a broad consensus that the United States and Britain failed to achieve either aim before, during and after the Iraq war of 2003. There were events on the ground that could not be explained: the failure to find any weapons of mass destruction, the chaos and carnage that followed the removal of Saddam Hussein's regime. These failures were made worse by the public diplomacy during the lead-up to war. The US and Britain had argued that intelligence showed Saddam's regime possessed an arsenal of chemical and biological weapons which posed a threat that could not be ignored. When none were found, the loss of public faith was disastrous. Meanwhile the prediction by the US Defense Secretary, Donald Rumsfeld, that Iraqis would gladly welcome Western troops was bloodily proved wrong by the appalling strife which followed.

These were misjudgements which future leaders contemplating conflict can be expected to study for a long time. The lessons are not necessarily straightforward. To those involved and working without hindsight (I was the Foreign Secretary's press secretary), it was unimaginable that any leader would choose conflict rather than open inspections if he no longer possessed illegal weapons. That Saddam's regime had possessed some chemical and biological weapons had been verified by international inspectors, but the Iraqi claim to have destroyed them was never open to verfication. So it would be too easy to say that a country should not go to war on a false prospectus – very obviously not. But what if government sincerely but mistakenly believes the prospectus is sound? Those who argue that it was wrong to rely on intelligence, for example in the British dossier, overlook that a previous Foreign Secretary, Lord Carrington, had to resign in 1982 because he took too little notice of intelligence that warned of an imminent invasion by Argentina of the Falkland Islands. That is a conundrum for policy-makers. The lesson for communicators is clearly that arguments based on intelligence can never again be sound public currency: there will always be the counter-argument that intelligence was wrong about Iraq.

But there should also be some wariness about this, since there may come a situation in which credible intelligence has to be acted on. For example, intelligence might point to a terrorist attack specifically enough for government to act pre-emptively. This would have to be explained, and this could be done only by reference to intelligence. It briefly appeared that this might have been the case before the bombing of a discotheque in Bali in 2002. Comments by the Foreign Minister of Australia – the country with the most victims – seemed to suggest that his and therefore the British government had had intelligence that warned of the Bali attack, but failed to act. In fact, a cool review of the intelligence – resisting the temptation to rush out denials that might turn out to be false – showed that the intelligence had referred to a possible attack on a tourist venue somewhere in South-East Asia, over an area far too wide for it to be practical to clear all tourist destinations until further notice. In this case, the intelligence had to be referred to publicly, once it had become the issue. This is clearly different from volunteering public arguments about possible future actions, based on intelligence. But it is a reminder that a rule against referring to intelligence cannot hold absolutely, in practice.

The problem remains. When a threat is diffuse and has its origins far from a country's shores – in other words, is not immediately visible – then a military response requires public trust as well as consent. Governments need to work harder to earn that trust, to show why action is needed and also to be honest about the risks. But 'making the case' risks having explanation shade into advocacy. One of the mistakes made by the UK on Iraq was to take on the burden of proof that Saddam Hussein's regime still possessed the illegal weapons which inspectors had verified some years before. The simple lesson here is that government should not seek to prove what it cannot be certain of. Over-statement is always a tactical mistake as well as being unjustifiable.

Some might argue that strategic communications – spokesmanship – has no place in war. But the Kosovo conflict is a case against this. The 78-day campaign was conducted amid media and public doubt about the war aim. It was government's duty, in a democracy, to articulate its aim. It was not as straightforward a war aim as defending your own country's borders from attack. This did not make the war wrong, only that serious attention needed to be paid to justifying it.

There was a strong sense in government that a previous Balkan tragedy, in Bosnia, should have been prevented by a more robust European and American intervention, if necessary military. The genocide in Rwanda was seen as another terrible example of people dying for lack of international intervention. But even if these examples were taken as valid arguments for acting differently in those circumstances, what was it about Kosovo that made it the right place to intervene? And even if there was a moral case – which many did not agree – there was the question of national interest: how could oppression by one of the world's many dictators far from British borders be described as a national interest? And then there was the important tactical question – could the aim be achieved? The consensus of commentators was that a bombing campaign could not succeed because there was no precedent for military victory by bombing, without ground troops being deployed.

In his broadcast to the nation at the start of hostilities, Tony Blair said: 'To those who say the aim of military strikes is not clear, I say it is crystal clear. It is to curb Slobodan Milosovic's ability to wage war on an innocent civilian population.' This did not answer the question why this dictator, why this country, but the reference to 'an innocent civilian population' gave a clear – though not unarguable – moral purpose. Robin Cook, the Foreign Secretary, told the Commons:

'Not to have acted, when we knew the atrocities that were being committed, would have been to make ourselves complicit in their repression.'

This moral case, which made no reference to direct British interests, ran into immediate difficulties when the first impact of the military campaign was a humanitarian crisis. The Serb leadership responded to NATO's attack by increasing its 'war on an innocent civilian population' with an intensity that drove many thousands to flee across the border into Macedonia.

The NATO governments involved in the campaign found themselves under criticism for apparently worsening the oppression they were supposed to be preventing, while triggering a refugee crisis that would not have existed but for the attacks. Whether or not President Milosevic calculated the media impact, the result of his immediate response on the ground was to produce a major crisis of legitimacy for the democratic governments ranged against him.

The particular problem of dealing with such a crisis of public diplomacy in the British media-political environment was illustrated by a front page headline in one of the Sunday newspapers invited to a briefing to explain government policy. This claimed that a senior British source had admitted the operation was a failure. In fact, the official concerned, who was not a politician and therefore had no experience of briefing under such pressures, had talked about a 'failure of imagination': that is, NATO had been unable to get inside the mind of a dictator capable of provoking a humanitarian crisis – it was unimaginable. The word 'failure' is rarely safe to use in any context in the presence of hostile journalists. (Not all journalists are hostile, it must be added: many wish to understand and explain, not misunderstand and misquote). By now the British government was in serious difficulty, with both its war aims and its competence to achieve them under attack.

The British government responded in two ways. On the ground, Robin Cook brokered NATO agreement and secured Macedonia's approval to create an area on Macedonian soil that would for current purposes not be regarded as sovereign Macedonia, but a United Nations safe haven for the refugees. This avoided Macedonia's great fear of being overwhelmed by a refugee population trying to settle permanently. By acting decisively and announcing the policy with promptness and clarity, the Foreign Secretary began to allay fears that NATO had got into a conflict whose consequences it could not cope with.

The second problem was to deal with the public diplomacy of the war. With so many states involved in the NATO alliance, there was also scope for division – real or apparent – that the media could feed upon, and for which the remedy was strong co-ordination. Robin Cook and the Defence Secretary, George Robertson, agreed to hold a daily press conference, turn and turn about, timed in late morning to reach US breakfast television and the British lunchtime bulletins, ahead of the daily NATO press conference held by its spokesman Jamie Shea in early afternoon. Shea would then pick up its theme in his early afternoon briefing, and then the US State Department briefing would do so three or four hours later. This meant there would be some coherence, and that difficult issues raised in one briefing could be passed on and dealt with in a co-ordinated way by subsequent briefings across NATO.

This required a high degree of international co-ordination, using machinery that had to be created right away. Alastair Campbell, the Prime Minister's spokes-man, went to NATO to help Jamie Shea set up the kind of office that is needed to service a daily press conference on events as fast-moving as a military conflict, drawing on press officers from across NATO. To co-ordinate ministe-rial statements and interviews, a daily conference call of spokespeople was set up between the US, Britain, France, Germany and Italy. Those five spokespeople, of whom I was the British, agreed recommendations to make to our five ministers, who began holding a daily conference call a little later in the afternoon. While communications was only one item on their agenda, it was established that the public diplomacy must be steered from the highest level. The public diplomacy had to be taken more seri-ously and dealt with more professionally. This could be done only if ministers were co-ordinating daily, drawing on advice from co-ordinated spokespeople. As Alastair Campbell noted in his diary of April 12 1999, on setting up the spokesmen's daily call: 'I emphasised they had to make sure there were people on there who were properly plugged in, not just space-fillers'. No communications work can be done effectively in government unless the communications advisors and/or spokespeople are 'prop-erly plugged in'. This is far from always the case. During those 'quint' calls, as they became known, it was often clear that some on the line had little or no access to or knowledge of their ministers' thinking. But some did, and as the usefulness of the co-ordinated communications became clear, so it became obvious that the daily quint calls were being taken more seriously in all capitals. The discipline of the daily quint call generated separate calls earlier in the day – among some of its participants, and with Jamie Shea – that increased the professionalism of the preparation and delivery of NATO's strategic communications.

The discipline of the daily press conference in London generated a much higher degree of thinking in government about what to say in justifying the military action day by day. This was an instrument of democracy, offering the world's media the chance to put questions on live television to the Foreign or Defence Secretary, who was always accompanied by the Chief of the Defence Staff, Sir Charles Guthrie, or one of the senior military figures who briefed the two ministers on the progress of the campaign every morning. Those briefings in the Ministry of Defence were held with an acute awareness among military and diplomatic personnel that one of their ministers was going to be held to account upstairs in the press conference room within a couple of hours.

Accountability was intensely difficult when NATO mistakenly bombed the Chinese embassy in Belgrade. This happened in the middle of the night as Robin Cook prepared to host a visit by the Russian Foreign Minister, Igor Ivanov. It was essential to maintain the tolerance if not the active support of Russia, which regarded the Balkans as an area of strategic interest, and whose permanent membership of the United Nations Security Council gave it a veto over any UN involvement. Robin Cook had established warm personal relations with Igor Ivanov. The Foreign Secretary invited him to spend the weekend in Edinburgh, during which they would hold a joint press conference to emphasise points of agreement and build mutual confidence.

Cook's team woke to the news that Igor Ivanov had understandably cancelled his visit in protest. The Foreign Secretary was due on the *Today* programme. There were no facts or explanation available, only the inexcusable reality of the bombing. Robin Cook decided the only way to deal with this terrible situation was to say sorry immediately, indeed to make sure he said sorry before the interviewer demanded it of him. This was not as easy as it may sound. Such interviews are tough even without a disaster to hand. Cook himself had had a bruising first year as Foreign Secretary, during which a series of media problems (rather than problems of policy substance) had cast doubt on his ability to survive in the job. He was still repairing his political credibility. Personally, he was a sensitive man who found dealing with the media more painful than his sharp-witted Commons performances would suggest; not the type of minister to brush a problem aside with a knockabout interview and move on. He was very painfully aware of the wrongness of what had happened in the night, even if it was accidental. On that, he had to take care, because although he found it inconceivable that NATO would do such a thing deliberately, he had at that time of the morning no evidence on which to draw. The interview had to be about saying sorry and no more.

A lesson of this difficult episode in a radio car in a rainy Edinburgh backstreet is that painful interviews should not be ducked purely because they are painful. Fault should not be sidestepped. Apologies should be prompt, full and dignified. Since this is not a book on domestic politics, it is not the place to look at the cases of ministers who might have saved their careers had they conducted themselves with the humility and dignity of Robin Cook that day.

Referring back to Iraq, when it became clear that there were no weapons of mass destruction, the then Foreign Secretary, Jack Straw, decided not to duck the issue. Instead, he devoted one morning to offering interviews in every outlet possible, as a way of acknowledging rather than sidestepping the fault. A government has every right to choose when to speak and when to be silent – and sometimes silence is the right policy, especially when facts are still being established – but it is a good rule that a democratic politician should answer for his actions in Parliament and the media unless there is a good tactical reason why not. Ministers are entitled to have a sense of timing in their interviews and announcements. But in general it is both good tactics and good

The difficulty of reconciling the challenges presented by different audiences sometimes leads to deliberate ambiguity. Arguably, Britain's relationship with the European Union has been a study in constructive ambiguity over several decades. But while ambiguity has legitimate uses, clarity is often a strategic necessity. This is the case either in setting benchmarks for international negotiations or, with higher stakes, in making clear the thresholds of a country's tolerance in a situation of potential conflict. The danger of failing to set clear thresholds for conflict is examined in a case study on India and Pakistan. The setting of benchmarks is discussed in a case study on European negotiations, and also features in the Israeli case study. A fourth general principle is that a country should define its international strategy by setting clear benchmarks or thresholds, unless a case can be proven for ambiguity. This is not only a tactical imperative, but a democratic one. A democracy is entitled to an explanation of the country's objectives, with expectations realistically set in advance, and outcomes justified.

Countries are different from individuals or companies and have different obligations when describing objectives and strategies. Governments need consent, whether that is active consent through the ballot box and checked by a free media, or passively, by proceeding on a given course unless the public makes it untenable. Consent requires explanation, so setting benchmarks is an instrument of domestic consent as well as of international bargaining.

A fifth general principle is that governments have a duty to explain. Even those who do not face re-election can face a catastrophic loss of public confidence. This is, in fact, the founding principle. Although it applies most obviously to democratic states, the duty to explain is a discipline that undemocratic regimes are unwise to ignore. One example in the case studies is the pressure that Iran has at times felt to pay heed to international opinion in the unfinished public diplomacy battle over its nuclear intentions. Failure to explain government actions – or taking actions with no justifiable explanation – was a thread running through the popular challenge to Arab dictators in 2011.

Objectives and evaluation

The emphasis on perceptions alongside reality makes the business of setting objectives and evaluating success more complex. In mainstream diplomacy, governments can set specific aims and be fairly clear if they have been achieved – though knowing what would have happened if they had acted differently is still usually a matter of informed guesswork. When dealing with perceptions, we need different tools, and the measurement of public opinion through surveys and qualitative tools such as in-depth interviews or media monitoring is essential. Used intelligently, these techniques can establish what different audiences (both whole populations and significant groups such as opinion-formers or international investors) democratic practice to be prompt. And when there is fault to be admitted, it is best done swiftly. Most fair-minded people, including most in the media, respect a prompt admission of fault.

The bombing of the Chinese embassy was only the most difficult of many incidents in the Kosovo conflict. It is not enough in international communications during a prolonged and major event like a military conflict to handle incidents professionally (crucial though that is). There needs to be a compelling narrative. It was noted above how Tony Blair and Robin Cook made a moral case for not standing aside while innocent civilians suffered, though without clarity on why Kosovo?

Tony Blair eventually articulated a narrative with his speech outlining a 'new doctrine of international community' on 22 April, a month into the conflict. In this, he said: 'We cannot turn our backs on conflicts and the violation of human rights within other countries if we want still to be secure.' It was as open-ended as John Kennedy's inaugural address: 'We shall pay any price, bear any burden, meet any hardship, support any friend, oppose any foe to assure the survival and success of our liberty.'

Blair, still under pressure to clarify his war aims, said that success was his only exit strategy. This was the utterly pragmatic counterweight to the moral element of the Blair doctrine, which became widely known as the doctrine of liberal intervention. As such, it was deemed to have been discredited when four years later Blair's sense of international community was one of the spurs to action in Iraq. There is a limit to what words can achieve, not only in achieving objectives but in defining them. The inescapable fact about intervention is that no doctrine can hold in all circumstances, since there will always be an element of choice and calculation, about the current attitudes and strengths of various leaders, and also about the intensity of media and parliamentary outrage about the oppression going on in a particular country. A doctrine which frankly weighed all the factors might go like this: a coalition of like-minded countries will intervene where they take a serious moral judgement that innocent lives must be saved, where it is deemed militarily practical to do so, and where there is a degree of public outrage that justifies the country's commitment and risk of its armed forces. The words 'judgement', 'deemed' and 'outrage' show how subjective such a doctrine must be. And where there is subjectivity, there is argument, and therefore the obligation on government to make its case.

Blair's original formulation about protecting 'innocent civilians' was arguably vindicated at the end of the conflict, when Kosovan leaders came out of hiding now that their lives were no longer in danger and told Robin Cook that they never lost hope because of his press conferences – he could not possibly speak so strongly day after day and then let them down.

The most important function of public diplomacy during conflict is for governments to meet their duty to justify the reasons for war and describe clear war aims; then to advance those aims. Governments should not seek to prove what cannot be certain, though they are entitled to make arguments that they sincerely believe to be true. Arguments based on intelligence will always be open to objection, following the Iraq experience. But neither can it be an absolute rule that governments do not refer to intelligence, if intelligence is the trigger for action. The best approach (suggested with humility, based on hard experience) is that efforts should be maintained to explain the limits of what is knowable, and the balance of judgement involved in weighing the evidence. Such restrained public communication is hardest under pressure and there is no greater pressure than war. But this pressure should not be an excuse, rather a spur to even higher standards than usual.

When several countries take part in joint military operations, special arrangements must be made to co-ordinate public diplomacy, however difficult it is to align a number of democracies with different cultures and perhaps different ideas of what justifies the war. This alignment needs to be done within the disciplines of the news cycle, so that decisions are speedy enough to make public information as up to date as possible. The conventional news cycle runs by mealtimes, from breakfast to lunch, through the afternoon to the early evening bulletins and then to the main bulletins in late evening, overnight into the breakfast bulletins and so on. This rhythm is complicated by the live updates on newspaper websites, by 24-hour television news and by the blizzard of informal reporting on ever more sophisticated handheld devices (the word 'telephone' hardly describes them). Though technological advances have speeded up the flow of news, the old-fashioned landmarks of bulletins watched by and newspapers read by millions still have impact.

Leaders must take seriously their duty to explain, and empower senior officials to organise coherent public diplomacy, not delegate this as a relatively unimportant task. This is important not only for the sake of a country doing all it can to achieve its legitimate objectives, but for a democratic reason too. A serious effort to justify military action day by day helps to make leaders accountable to the public.

Inevitably, mistakes are made. When this happens, there should be a prompt, full and dignified apology. At all times take care to establish the facts, and not to make statements which are not yet supported by complete knowledge of the facts. Where facts are confused or slow to be established, confine statements to what is certain: and be publicly clear about that. Governments are entitled to choose their timing, and sometimes silence is prudent, but the default assumption must be full and prompt disclosure, within the bounds of militarily operational effectiveness, for example not disclosing information that would put forces' lives at risk or jeopardise operations.

Chapter Seven

Iran

In 2003, reports from the International Atomic Energy Agency aroused concern that Iran was seeking the capacity to produce nuclear weapons. The foreign ministers of Britain, France and Germany decided to make a discreet joint approach in writing to the foreign minister of Iran. Kamal Kharazzi wrote back, inviting Jack Straw, Dominque de Villepin and Joschka Fischer to Tehran. While they hoped the Iranian regime genuinely wanted dialogue, they feared that Tehran saw their joint approach as a public relations opportunity to be exploited. Should the three make a joint visit? If so what were the risks of Iran using them not to start a serious discussion but for some sort of diplomatic game as cover for continuing to develop its nuclear technology? Would an EU intervention provide a means of resolving the problem diplomatically, or a means for Iran to prevaricate while developing its technology?

The decision was taken to accept the risk and travel warily, sharing with the media the IAEA's public reports (not intelligence) which were cause for concern, and drawing attention to the possible breaches of the Nuclear

Non-Proliferation Treaty, to which Iran was a signatory. This was soon after the invasion of Iraq, and there was no military threat in the approach of the 'EU3', rather an emphasis on wishing to come to agreement with Iran on the limits of activities under the treaty. This was a highly technical matter, involving the installation of centrifuges capable of producing grades of uranium unnecessary for civil nuclear power, but also usable in nuclear weapons. Without mastering all the detail of this complex subject, it was necessary for all present to understand that centrifuges are used to spin uranium gas, filtering it down to the 'richest' form, from the point of view of producing weapons grade material.

A risk to be avoided was coming to an ambiguous agreement which Iran could exploit to continue a level of activity that might enable it to pass an irrevocable threshold of technical capability. The Iranian government might use a joint press conference to imply consent for its activities, so any agreement needed to be clear in its meaning, setting a benchmark which could be readily understood and not creatively re-interpreted.

At the critical moment in the negotiation, the Iranian side proposed an agreement to 'suspend uranium enrichment', which was the technical development causing the main concern. The EU side insisted that the phrase 'suspension of enrichment activities' was necessary. The reason for this was that Iran's phrase would prohibit only the act of enrichment, not the installation of the centrifuges which do the enriching. The EU phrase was intended to suspend the building of centrifuges – the capacity, as well as the production.

Both sets of negotiators made clear to one another that they should not emerge with a text that each immediately interpreted in different ways, making it meaningless and bringing this peaceful means of resolving the issue into disrepute. It was essential to agree a yardstick by which to judge Iran's future actions. However, during a recess in the talks, the EU ministers felt they were being used as cover for an agreement which would allow Iran to continue developing its capacity while appearing to co-operate with the international community. This had been their fear all along. In contrast to many anodyne communiqués, the words to be agreed that day were not about presentation but were themselves the substance, in a moment of potentially dangerous international disagreement.

It became known to the British team at this stage that the Iranian hosts had set up a joint press conference for their own and the British, French and German media. At the EU preparation breakfast, it had been agreed that the EU ministers should appear jointly with the Iranians only if there were a satisfactory agreement. So when the negotiations resumed, the British Foreign Secretary told the Iran negotiator that there would be no press conference unless it was to publish a text including the phrase 'suspension of enrichment activities'. This point was then conceded. So the Iranian tactic of using talks and a joint press conference to obtain an exploitable agreement was turned against the host, who decided not to risk the fiasco of being stood up. At the press conference, the EU ministers decided not to over-state the case by talking of a 'successful outcome', since the outcome could be tested only by whether Iran delivered. Instead, the three ministers agreed to confine themselves to talking merely of 'progress'. This had the added virtue of not making the press conference difficult for the Iranian negotiator, Hassan Rouhani (regarded as a restraining influence within the Iranian leadership).

Another point about the press conference was that the British media had been long prepared for this moment. When it first became clear that the EU might make an intervention, the Foreign Office organised a series of briefings with senior officials to go through the technical and diplomatic issues with correspondents likely to be covering the issue. This was done in twos and threes so that these conversations could be serious, low-key and factual. This depended on relationships of mutual respect between journalists and officials. It was stressed that no decisions had been taken about how to deal with the problem – and the visit was not announced until the last minute – but correspondents appreciated the effort to help them grasp a complex subject in good time, and to realise that this was soon going to become an important news story. This produced a dividend at the press conference, where the British spokespeople were able to point quickly and plausibly to key passages in the text, to journalists who had known for some time what the British approach was going to be.

Iran did suspend enrichment activities for a period, though they were resumed and, as of mid-2012, the issue remains unresolved. But the EU3 visit to Tehran was the one moment in this saga in which diplomacy achieved a sensible outcome, despite the high risk of confrontation. It also shows how media activity around an international negotiation can be used as a tool of diplomacy, if each side's desire for a presentable outcome is used with skill by the negotiators. Equally, there is a risk that it can be a tool used against negotiators who fail to see its importance and find themselves being exploited publicly by an opponent. Getting this right cannot be done unless the media understands (a) the issues under negotiation, (b) your objectives, (c) the dangers if those objectives are not achieved, (d) your minimum outcome. This takes a good deal of work in advance, based on long-term relationships of respect. Prepare the media by explaining the technical background and the political imperatives – it is worth the time and the risk (of misinterpretation, for example). This builds mutual respect and helps ensure that outcomes are credible, when judged against the earlier briefings on background. Serious reporters do not expect to be told everything. They do expect to be trusted with your overall assessment of the information available and with a reasonably frank analysis of your negotiating strategy, while understanding that any negotiator must reserve some privacy for his or her negotiating hand. So on point (d) – minimum outcome – the spokesperson needs to give the media a realistic sense of what matters in the outcome, and how to judge it. If government does not give such an assessment, then the media – or an opponent – will set expectations where they choose. If so, the bar will usually be set too high.

Sometimes, when the chances of success are low, it is worth being blunt about that. During Britain's EU presidency in 2005, there was a difficult negotiation over terms for Turkey's accession, strongly opposed by Austria, with a serious prospect of deadlock. Reporters travelling with the Foreign Secretary – including documentary-makers with generous access – were told they might very well be watching one of the great British failures. In fact, the outcome was narrowly a success – uncertain to the end – and credit was given in the media because of the openness shown in describing the difficulties beforehand. This has to be genuine, not a bluff. On that occasion, as with the nuclear talks in Tehran, the media made its own judgement that the difficulties were real, not a game of lowering expectations. This is the point about relationships of trust. The sort of issues dealt with in high level negotiations tend to be reported by correspondents who will be there next time, and again and again, so they quickly realise who is playing games, and who is trying to help them understand and report accurately. There is a great temptation in government not to treat the media as serious partners. Journalists do of course have different objectives, but also a common interest in public information. Despite the excesses of some, it cannot be underlined too heavily that building relationships of mutual respect with the media is essential. The other aspect of trust – afterwards, as well as before – is the necessity to avoid over-stating outcomes. Over-statement may earn a day or two's relatively good coverage, but there is no forgiveness when the reality emerges. This is especially true where – as in the Tehran talks – agreements are dependent on delivery over time.

Chapter Eight

Israel and Palestine

The Palestinian application for membership of the United Nations set overlapping public diplomacy challenges for Israel and the United States, for members of the Security Council, for the European Union's new institutional arrangements for common foreign policy, for Arab countries; and for the Palestinians themselves.

In fact, the Palestinian approach to the UN was more an act of public diplomacy than of diplomacy itself, since there was little to be gained in substance. Once the US made clear, well in advance, that it would veto Palestinian membership of the UN, there was no chance of the Palestinians achieving that aim. But there was much to be won or lost in shifting the balance of strategic advantage between Palestine and Israel. For all of the participants, especially the US, there was much more at stake than a technical upgrade in Palestine's status at the UN. America's standing in the Arab world at a moment of great change; its credibility as a champion of democracy and as a country with ideals; and its ability to act as guarantor to Israel by dictating the terms of this strategically pivotal conflict – all were at risk. For Israel, the Palestinian campaign presented a serious challenge, whatever the procedural outcome. Even if Israel won a tactical victory by thwarting the UN bid, it might suffer long-term strategic loss if the campaign increased its international isolation.

The situation was this. After abortive negotiations sponsored by President Obama in September 2010, the Palestinian leadership decided to try a different approach to achieving independent statehood than had been pursued since the 'Oslo' agreements signed by Yasser Arafat and Yitzhak Rabin in 1993. The Palestinians would 'head to the UN', as President Abbas put it, at the annual ministerial meeting of the General Assembly. There was ambiguity – confusion at times – over what specifically the Palestinians intended to achieve and by what means at the UN. But the big fact established over the summer of 2011 was that the whole international community was going to be asked to make some sort of decision about the Israeli-Palestinian dispute.

By 'heading to the UN' – whatever that meant in practice – the Palestinian leadership hoped to change their situation in the following ways.

1. The peace process the Palestinians would no longer be confined within the boundaries of the long-established 'Oslo' process, which they judged to have failed to deliver their objective of statehood. European and Arab countries would be obliged to take their own positions, facing up to dilemmas long ignorable thanks to the seemingly unending US-dominated peace process.

2. The Arab Spring instead of being ignored amid the dramas of the Arab awakening, the Palestinian problem would be seen as an issue which needed re-assessing and dealing with differently in the context of enormous regional change. President Abbas used his UN speech to call for a 'Palestinian Spring', linking the Palestinian cause to other Arab freedom movements.

3. Israel's strategic posture Israel's relatively comfortable position as occupying power, presenting itself as a willing negotiator unable to find a partner, would be subjected to critical worldwide scrutiny.

These potential gains of substance in Palestine's situation and prospects were all pursued by statements, not action: through international strategic communications as a means of advancing national interests in pursuit of strategic objectives.

Let's look at the public diplomacy challenges facing the participants in turn: the United States under President Barack Obama; Israel under Prime Minister Binyamin Netanyahu; the Palestine Liberation Organisation, the UN-recognised body representing the Palestinian people chaired by Mahmoud Abbas (who was also President of the Palestinian Authority, which administers the occupied territory); and the wider Arab and Muslim world.

The United States

President Obama came to office amid high expectations and goodwill, which he fuelled in the Arab world by making an early speech that seemed to promise a new approach to the Middle East. As far as it went, this was a triumph of public diplomacy. But it was soon clear that it lacked substance in action. When the Israeli government defied Obama's call for a halt to building in the settlements during negotiations, the Arab world was disappointed by the US President's retreat. America's approval ratings in the Arab world quickly subsided from relatively high levels, back where they had been, or lower. This was the inevitable, even predictable, consequence of fine words that were not seen through in action.

The change in views of the US was charted among others by the Arab American Institute, which said in a commentary on a poll conducted by Zogby International in mid-2011: 'With the 2008 election of Barack Obama, favorable attitudes toward the U.S. more than doubled in many Arab countries. But in the two years since his famous "Cairo speech," ratings for both the U.S. and the President have spiraled downwards. The President is seen overwhelmingly as failing to meet the expectations set during his speech, and the vast majority of those surveyed disagree with U.S policies. In five out of the six countries surveyed, the U.S. was viewed less favorably than Turkey, China, France – or Iran. Far from seeing the U.S. as a leader in the post-Arab Spring environment, the countries surveyed viewed "U.S. interference in the Arab world" as the greatest obstacle to peace and stability in the Middle East, second only to the continued Palestinian occupation......'

According to the international opinion research firm Pew '...many of the concerns that have driven animosity toward the U.S. in recent years are still present – a perception that the U.S. acts unilaterally, opposition to the war on terror, and fears of America as a military threat. And in countries such as Jordan, Lebanon, and Pakistan, most say their own governments co-operate too much with the U.S.'

The uprisings known as the Arab Spring therefore took off at a time when the US President had little goodwill in the region, and limited scope for speaking credibly in support of democracy and self-determination, partly because he was seen as having failed to promote either in the Palestinian case. James Zogby's commentary on the Arab American Institute poll said: 'Obama's performance ratings are lowest on the two issues to which he has devoted the most energy: Palestine and engagement with the Muslim world'.

Each revolution presented the US President with contradictory imperatives – to support democratic movements, while worrying about regional stability; to stand by allies while respecting self-determination; and to celebrate Arab freedom while concerned about the possible emergence of extreme Islamic revolutionary leaderships. For a large proportion of humanity – Arabs and Muslims – America was going to be judged in 2011 by the way it responded to Middle East democracy and self-determination.

The importance of the Palestinian issue to many in the Arab world was illustrated by Zogby's poll for the Arab American Institute. Asked to choose the issue on which Americas could do most to improve ties with the Arab world, 73% of Egyptians chose resolving the Palestinian issue, 60% of Jordanians, and 58% of Moroccans. In Lebanon, the issue came second (33%) to ending the Iraq war (34%), while in Kuwait it was third (14%) behind engaging with the Muslim world (20%) and efforts to stop Iran's nuclear programme (51%).

This was the difficult context for the White House as the PLO pushed its own bid for self-determination to the top of the agenda in September. America could not champion Arab freedom while voting against Palestinian statehood at the UN, without seeming inconsistent to Arab publics. While myriad actions and statements over long periods add up to national definition, the US was going to make a major statement about itself by the way its conduct at the UN was perceived around the world in the face of the Palestinian challenge. This had wider reso- nance than in the Middle East, since the Israeli-Palestinian issue arouses strong feelings perhaps more widely across the world than any other, given the religious and historic significance of the land subject to dispute.

President Obama was obviously not focused solely on his standing in the Muslim world in deciding his policy on the Palestinian UN bid. Opinion in Israel and among American Jews (not the same thing) matters to any US President. Obama was often reported to be in difficulty with both constituencies, though some of this reporting was excessively influenced by partisan commentators. It was often reported that President Obama's allegedly weak support for Israel was apparently costing the Democrats support among American Jews. In fact, according to Gallup, the President's declining approval among Jewish voters closely matched his overall decline among the whole US electorate, so was likely to have more to do with wider economic and other concerns than with issues related specifically to Israel.

In Israel, President Obama's standing was not as big a problem as some media commentators suggested. For example, in May 2011 a study by the New American Foundation 'found that 41% of Israelis have favorable views of Obama, while 37% view him unfavorably'. That standing '...is notably stronger than opinion toward the Israeli Defense and Foreign Ministers, and his unfavorable rating is only four points higher than the unfavorable rating for his predecessor, George W. Bush.' This was not the impression to be gained from regular reading of much of the Israeli media.

This is an illustration of the way that even the measures of public diplomacy – such as polls – can be used in a partisan way to influence the atmosphere in which decisions are taken. Decisions are not necessarily made entirely rationally on the basis of objective evidence, but to an extent by instinct and perception, influenced by anxiety and pressure. There is always scope for perceptions to be shaped by partial reading of statistics or by a certain interpretation of the figures being played up by the media or by energetic political advocates. Only a tiny fraction of those reading a dramatic headline would think to check the survey results themselves.

Government can challenge this by setting out clearly and with confidence its own understanding of ambiguous facts. The ambiguity in this case was that while President Obama was not overwhelmingly popular among Jews, neither was he doing especially badly, and the reasons for his poll numbers were open to different interpretations. There was no straight line connecting his support among Jewish voters in New York or Florida to the issue of Palestinian statehood. But there was an atmosphere, fostered by noisy advocacy, that made Israel-Palestine a domestic issue as well as a foreign policy dilemma.

President Obama might have handled the Palestinian UN bid differently had he chosen to stress the importance of raising US standing in the Arab world while having his team underline the comparative steadiness of Jewish support at a time of wider difficulty for the President. But the Congressional and media opposition to the Palestinian campaign was not challenged by the US administration, which seemed content with the impression that going against the Israel government on this issue was outside the reasonable range of policy options. President Obama's statement of support for Palestinian membership at the previous UN General Assembly only a year before was dropped from the Presidential script. This was a choice – the President could have emphasised his determination to stick by what he had said, if he had so chosen. But President Obama chose to be influenced by the perception that he was in trouble with the Jewish vote, compounding his far greater difficulties in Congress over the US economy.

It is impossible to say what decisions President Obama might have taken amid political silence on the issue. The reality was that he took his decisions amid a combination of vigorous Israeli advocacy and strong hostility in Congress to supporting the Palestinians at the UN, in a media-political environment that assumed he could not afford to offend an important domestic constituency. His decision not to challenge this was a strategic choice, of substance, not presentation. Its impact was two-fold. First, nobody doubted that Palestinian statehood would be blocked at the UN. Second, Israel was under no pressure to compensate by making serious proposals for negotiation towards Palestinian statehood. Once President Obama had retreated in the face of Binyamin Netanyahu's public relations campaign, the Israeli PM felt secure in his chosen position: saying that the only way forward was direct bilateral negotiation, while ensuring there was no progress towards such a negotiation. Between one September and the next, 2010 to 2011, President Obama's Israel-Palestine policy was checkmated by Israel's public diplomacy.

Israel

Prime Minister Binyamin Netanyahu had at first been uncharacteristically slow to see the public diplomacy challenge posed by the Palestinian move to the UN, perhaps over-estimating two important matters of substance.

The first was his real-world grasp of the impotence of the UN to change facts on the ground in Israel and occupied Palestine. Whatever decision might be taken in New York, it would not result in a single checkpoint being removed or settlement being dismantled unless Israel so chose. And Israel had shown over more than 40 years its indifference to UN resolutions calling for an end to the occupation; those steps that Israel had taken towards peace during those decades had come through other channels and in response to other pressures or incentives. The second was his hard-headed reading of US politics, that Congress was so strongly supportive of Israel that the Palestinians could not put serious countervailing pressure on the White House by any means, including a UN vote. Mr Netanyahu understood that Congress is not frightened by UN disapproval, and indeed was prepared to threaten funding for any UN agency which recognised Palestine. (This threat was duly carried out in respect of Unesco in 2011.)

The Israeli Prime Minister even signalled that he would not go to the UNGA, but delegate the task to President Peres, before realising his tactical error. Of course, the facts would not change 'the day after' a UN vote, as most commentators pointed out, but the Israeli PM came to see that the context for imposing facts might change to his disadvantage, over time, if the Palestinians managed to weaken international support for Israel. So he set his own benchmarks for victory or defeat, to ensure that he could deny the Palestinian leadership any advantage.

It was not clear until shortly before the meeting whether the PLO would go to the 15-nation Security Council to ask for full membership of the UN, against the certainty of a US veto; or go to the UN General Assembly, where all 192 nations would make a decision on a majority vote, with no-one having a veto. While the PLO was likely to win a majority at UNGA, the Assembly could not grant full membership of the UN, only an upgrade of Palestine's status as an observer. The Israeli Prime Minister set as his main benchmark denying the Palestinians full membership through the Security Council: easily done, given the promised US veto. His second benchmark could not be denying the PLO a win at the Assembly as this was unachievable, so Binyamin Netanyahu instead emphasised the importance of Israel winning the support of around a third of the Assembly, including major countries in, for example, Europe. His implication that it would not matter to lose a majority of less important countries, as he defined them, had no basis in the UN rulebook, but reflected his grasp that Israel would not be under serious pressure to end the occupation unless it 'lost' the consensus among relatively powerful nations on whom it had always relied.

This tactic reflected Prime Minister Netanyahu's understanding of what was really at stake, whatever the outcome in terms of Palestinian status at the UN. This was a battle of legitimacy. He saw this as a zero-sum equation, in which any increase in Palestinian legitimacy was a loss of Israeli legitimacy. He chose not to define the issue in another way, that Israel might gain from increased Palestinian legitimacy, if Israel were seen to be acting as a partner in promoting the two-state solution through UN recognition. This alternative was advanced by some Israeli commentators, but it ran against the zero-sum strategy that the Prime Minister had most clearly set out in his speech to the US Congress in May.

The Israeli Prime Minister was given a rapturous reception when he spoke to Congress. This event was a significant act of international strategic communications allied to diplomacy, perhaps more important than the Palestinian UN move, if judged by likely impact on the immediate future for Israelis and Palestinians. It was the clearest possible demonstration that Israeli had an unbreakable hold on US decision-making. It is hard to think of an example of a leader of one country going into the heart of another's politics and showing his raw power there, as confidently as Mr Netanyahu did.

The Israeli Prime Minister felt strong enough to reject without any diplomatic disguise the initiative that President Obama had taken a few days before in calling for Israeli-Palestinian negotiations with, as their starting point, the border that had existed on the eve of the 1967 war. He gave his rejection not only in his speech to Congress, but most strikingly in a joint press conference during which he gave the US President a lecture on the realities as he, Mr Netanyahu, saw them. Nobody watching could remember a visiting leader – a supposedly friendly one – speaking to an American President in that way.

Mr Netanyahu declared the 1967 border to be 'indefensible' and within days President Obama had re-worked his formula in Israel's favour. (The phrase '1967 border' is part of the jargon of the Middle East Peace Process, shorthand for the situation that existed before Israel invaded and occupied Palestine, as the Arab world sees it, or acted in self-defence as Israel sees it; leaving the West Bank as disputed territory as Israel sees it, or land occupied in defiance of international law, as the relevant UN resolutions define it.) President Obama now said the border was bound to be different, thus releasing Mr Netanyahu from any obligation to use 1967 as the baseline.

This episode contributed to the strategic weakening of the President's position in the Arab world, and strengthened the Israeli government's conviction that it could maintain the status quo without concessions, whatever initiatives the Palestinians might try. Thus a series of three speeches (Obama-Netanyahu-Obama) had an impact on the substance: US intervention to pressure Israeli concessions and trigger a genuine negotiation became impossible because Mr Netanyahu had appealed over the President to Congress with dramatic success, and no penalties.

But the PLO move to the UN now threatened to place the dispute in a court of opinion much less favourable to Israel than the US Congress. Although Mr Netanyahu had locked up the only decision-making body with genuine power to change the situation – the US Congress – he saw the danger to Israel of losing support and respect among a critical mass of nations as the Palestinian leadership gained respect for its state-building efforts. There was an alternative approach that he might have taken to avoid this loss of respect and support, which was to welcome the widely applauded institutional and security reforms achieved by the PA government of Salam Fayyad, and to work with the Abbas-Fayyad partnership to bring a competent Palestinian state into independent existence while the opportunity lasted. But through every speech, interview and briefing, Mr Netanyahu made clear that the proposed alternative of working with the Palestinian leadership to achieve their independent statehood was beyond consideration.

By setting achievable benchmarks at the UN, Mr Netanyahu used that process to divert attention from the much bigger and for Israel more difficult issue of whether the Palestinian government actually was ready to run a viable state. Rather than engage in a potentially risky debate on what Israel's strategic approach should be to Palestinian statehood, he focused diplomatic and media attention on tactical questions – how much support for Palestine in the Assembly? Would the Palestinians get the nine votes in the Security Council necessary to force a US veto? Focusing world attention on second order tactical dramas is often used by skilled communicators to divert attention from first order issues. Mr Netanyahu was much more comfortable in September 2011 with a drama over UN voting than he would have been with the international focus being on a series of reports from the World Bank, IMF and others certifying that the Palestinian Authority had done everything necessary to be ready for statehood. This first order strategic question – in what respect if any did Palestine fall short of readiness for independence? – went mostly un-asked. This could be seen as a major strategic error by the PLO, giving Israel a battle in which it could define victory on its own terms; instead of a battle Israel could not win, to deny that Salam Fayyad's government had created a country ready for independence as defined by the UN, World Bank, IMF and European Union.

Equally, it could be argued that Fayyad's incremental and constructive approach was never going to force the critical decision-makers in the US to support Palestinian independence against Israel's wishes.

Palestinian leadership

Those who argued that the PLO move to the UN was mistaken overlooked the poor position that President Abbas would have been in had there been no Palestinian initiative in the wake of Mr Netanyahu's placing a Congressional deadlock on the peace process with his speech that ruled out any concession on any issue to be negotiated (borders, the status of Jerusalem, the return of refugees etc.) President Obama, battered by Congress over a much more domestically important issue that summer – the US deficit – would have had no incentive to re-enter the Israeli-Palestinian argument at this time, except that he had no choice but to find a means of handling the UN in September. It is unclear what alternatives Abbas and the PLO leadership had, except the 'doomsday' option of dissolving the Palestinian Authority itself.

Without the UN bid, Palestinian paralysis would have coincided with dramatic movement in some neighbouring countries. And the international community would have had no reason to divert attention from the urgency of developments in Egypt, Libya and Syria. But while creating their own sense of urgency, the Palestinian leadership did nothing to specify what outcome the move to the UN was meant to achieve.

The advantage of vagueness was that the international community had to respond to a general sense of 'action required' rather than be diverted into details about what precisely was going to be tabled at the UN. In fact, when the detail did surface, it was at first uncompelling, centring on whether the Palestinians might be upgraded into a status similar to the Vatican as a non-member state. Other detail proved dangerous to the Palestinian cause, for example the possibility that any upgrade might enable the Palestinians to take Israel to the International Criminal Court: anathema to the US and unwelcome in Europe, where there was no appetite for war crimes trials against the Israelis. So the PLO's imprecision – whether deliberate or a function of its tendency to speak with many voices – enabled the Palestinians to float into the UN meeting on a tide of sympathy, without its international supporters having had to make difficult choices.

The disadvantages included that allies did not know what they were being asked to do, and feared that when it came to it, they might be asked for more than they wanted to deliver. This was strongly felt in Europe, where Britain, for example, wanted to help the Palestinians achieve a good outcome, rejected the position the US was pushing within the Quartet (notably support for Palestinian recognition of an explicitly Jewish state), but feared that the PLO would not be content with the sort of compromise Britain could endorse.

Another disadvantage was that the PLO made no attempt to set benchmarks for success, as the Israelis did, although President Abbas made clear in his speech before departure for New York that the initiative was not intended to end the occupation immediately. This may sound obvious, but one problem for the Palestinian leadership had been that when Prime Minister Salam Fayyad was characteristically open about this in early summer, some took him to be dissenting from the official position. And there was concern that if the Palestinian public expected change, disappointment would lead to violence. In fact, polls in Palestine suggested a mature understanding that the UN move was not going to lift the occupation, and that there was little interest in returning to violence.

Prime Minister Fayyad's main contribution to the PLO strategy was to bring to fruition the government state-building programme in timely fashion, so that he and the President could quote the verdicts of the World Bank and others that the PA was now ready to govern a viable independent state, with internationally-respected standards of security and economic management.

Between them, Abbas and Fayyad had transformed the Palestinian appeal to the world, by linking the dry detail of financial management and service delivery to the wider narrative of Palestinian freedom, over a period that pre-dated the decision to move to the UN. Much of Salam Fayyad's programme was too technical for media or public consumption, but with the President's support he conveyed a sense of dynamic purpose through a reform agenda designed to over-ride Israel's traditional trump cards in public diplomacy – its own security concerns, and the perception of Palestinian mismanagement. This was a striking success for international strategic communications. There was an alternative perception of Palestine available to the world: that of division between Fatah and Hamas, with Gaza still a source of potential and sometimes actual violence against Israel. But, with the crucial exception of the US Congress, there was a growing respect among decision-makers and opinion-formers across the world for the competence of Palestinian government. This even permeated some of the US media, for example *The New York Times*, where columnist Thomas Friedman coined the term of praise 'Fayyadism' for a strategy of building support by building competent institutions. Even more important than financial competence was the value placed by many in the international community on the PA security reforms, which contributed to the quietest period on the West Bank for many years (a view shared by a leaked Israeli intelligence assessment).

But if Israel could no longer make the security argument with such conviction as before, the Palestinian leadership was still vulnerable to Mr Netanyahu's ability to portray them – rather than him – as the obstacle to negotiations. He portrayed himself as a man with no preconditions by the basic technique of simply saying so, again and again. Anybody involved in political communication at any level needs to remember the often neglected point that repetition is crucial. It would be too cynical to say that repetition trumps reality, but a simple message restated with consistency and conviction can go a long way to winning an argument by default. When the PA conducted some research among US opinion-formers in 2010, it found that one repeated message came through all the blizzard of argument and commentary about the situation – that Israel is 'the only democracy in the Middle East'. The Palestinians had no message that made any impact with this important audience, though media commentary in 2011 suggested that Salam Fayyad's reforms might have started to register with US opinion-formers.

While Prime Minister Netanyahu continued to present himself as ready for talks without condition, President Abbas never managed to articulate as simple a case as Mr Netanyahu for his own objection to negotiating while settlement building continued.

One problem for the Palestinians in this argument is the word 'settlement' itself. It is a small masterpiece of 'framing' an argument by the deliberate choice of language and associations: in this case, suggesting the harmless and homely creation of new communities in the wilderness, with its instinctive appeal to American audiences. Palestinian spokespeople use the word 'settlement' as if it is proof of Israel's determination to occupy rather than negotiate, without realising that the word has no pejorative connotations in western ears, except to the small minority versed in the detail of the dispute.

Lack of knowledge is an Israel public diplomacy asset. This can be illustrated by a column written by an English journalist who knows Israel and Palestine well, but who was shocked when taken to the West Bank city of Hebron to see the separation measures taken to keep Palestinians away from the settlers in the town. Jonathan Freedland wrote in the UK newspaper *The Jewish Chronicle* on 7 November 2011: 'What I saw there would shock even those who think they know all there is to know about Israel and its conflict with the Palestinians. The centre of a city of 175,000 people has been utterly emptied, its streets deserted, its shops vacant, thanks to a policy the Israeli army calls "sterilisation" – ensuring the area is clear and safe for Hebron's 800 Jewish settlers.' Similarly, a lack of knowledge of the impact of settlements on nearby Palestinian communities makes it harder for outsiders to appreciate the PLO position.

Freedland's piece was quoted approvingly by Roger Cohen in *The New York Times* in a commentary on a rare failure of Israeli public diplomacy in the US on 6 December 2011. As part of an advertising campaign appealing to Jews to immigrate, Israel caused anger by placing the ads in the United States. As Cohen described the campaign, it was 'intended to shame Israeli expatriates in the United States into returning home by suggesting that America is no place for real Jews and that Diaspora life leads to loss of Jewish identity. The Jewish Federations of North America called the ads "outrageous and insulting".' The ads were promptly withdrawn, leaving Roger Cohen in no doubt of the reason: 'The one true existential threat to Israel is loss of U.S. support – which will never happen...'

The strategic importance of Israel's image in the west was underlined by a critical columnist in the left-of-centre Israeli newspaper *Haaretz*, Ari Shavit, on 8 December 2011: 'Israel's base is the democratic West. Historically, the West created Israel. Politically, the West supported Israel. As for security, the West conferred on Israel its military strength. Economically, the strong connection with the West enabled the formation of a modern and prosperous Israeli economy. It's the democratic West that set up Israel and ensures its survival. Even when hostile legions besieged us, the stable base of the West's support defended us. The alliance with the United States and Europe has meant that no political failure, no military failure and no regional storm have undermined the Jewish state.... The democratic West now looks at Israel in disbelief.... This is our strategic home front. If we lose it, we will not survive. '

Shavit, referring to Ultra-Orthodox attitudes to women, as well as settlement building, understood the importance of knowledge that, from his point of view, was beginning to undermine Israel as it became more widespread, changing Israel's image for the worse. He was writing after US Defense Secretary Leon Panetta and Secretary of State Hillary Clinton both made unusually critical comments on Israel. While Panetta said it was time to 'get to the damn table', Clinton criticised the treatment of women by Ultra-Orthodox Jews in Israel, for example by segregating them from men on buses. This chimed with a conclusion drawn by Roger Cohen, that some Israeli expatriates of his acquaintance 'are troubled by the illiberal drift of Israeli politics, the growth of a harsh nationalism, the increasing influence of the ultrareligious, the endlessness of the "situation," and the tension inherent in a status quo that will one day threaten either Israel's Jewishness or its democracy.'

For all Mr Netanyahu's skill in Congress, here was evidence that a potentially sympathetic audience with detailed knowledge of the situation – US Jews – were more interested in facts on the ground. Public diplomacy does have limits. But unease about Israeli politics and culture did not translate at any point in 2011 into a serious effort to break the deadlock. Though much commentary going into the UN criticised Mr Netanyahu (notably in *The New York Times* and *Financial Times*), the consensus among decision-making and opinion-forming elites remained that the dispute could be resolved only through bilateral negotiation, not through the United Nations. So to that extent, Israeli public diplomacy still had the stronger grip. The pressure was going to be on President Abbas to be satisfied with a limited success at the UN in return for going into negotiations with an Israeli leader who still had the formidable asset of US backing.

So the question was whether President Abbas could force a role for the international community in the peace process which might at last turn the key in Palestinian favour, in a way that 20 years of US-brokered negotiations had not done. This was the real outcome of the UN bid which the Palestinian leadership wanted – creating a diplomatic crisis out of which would come a new process that would be more international, less subject to American mediation. President Abbas was undeterred by Congressional threats to cut funding to the PA if he proceeded, threats which hardened after Mr Netanyahu's triumph in May. This signalled a willingness by the PLO to take risks in the effort to break out of the Israeli-American hold on the peace process, and was thus a break with a Palestinian strategy which had throughout President Abbas' five-year leadership been framed by a reluctance to challenge the US. Mahmoud Abbas had even longer been the Palestinian most closely associated with the Middle East Peace Process, so his UN bid marked the transformation of a 20-year strategy. It was not entirely clear where the new strategy would lead, but what was clear was that President Abbas no longer saw bilateral meetings with Israel under US sponsorship as desirable or even politically tenable. If a negotiation was launched at the UN with a genuine Quartet role, Israel would be less able to stick to positions on borders and settlements, Jerusalem and refugees, than in talks solely sponsored by the US and mediated by officials who had been involved since Oslo.

The Arab and Muslim world

In 2011, the Arab world was more diverse than even a year before, with several major countries in mid-revolution, and all facing dilemmas produced by the Arab Spring. Each leadership was conscious of the Palestinian cause as a factor in domestic opinion (see above for variations between countries).

Egypt was the most directly affected by Israel-Palestine. Its own alliance with Israel was open to question as the country moved from dictatorship, by way of supposedly temporary military rule, towards democratic elections beginning soon after the UN General Assembly. Shortly before the UN meeting, Egyptian demonstrators besieged the Israeli embassy. This traumatic event for Israel, coupled with a serious rift in relations between Israel and Turkey, created a strong sense that the Arab and Muslim powers were disowning friendships with Israel as 'the street' showed its power. But Egypt, like Turkey, had an important relationship with the United States, as well as an interest in regional leadership. Prime Minister Erdogan of Turkey saw an opportunity to strengthen his country's regional position (including at the expense of Iran) by going to Cairo to speak at the Arab League meeting shortly before UNGA. There he described Israel as 'the West's spoiled child' and said it was an obligation to support the Palestinians at the UN. This speech was an example of communications as substance. No action was taken – only words from a podium – but Turkey had asserted itself at a moment of fluidity, forcing the US to take account of Ankara to a greater extent than it might have done over the whole range of its international activities, not just in relation to Israel-Palestine. Opposing the US was not risk-free for a member of NATO, but Prime Minister Erdogan seemed determined to forge a more assertive role for his country.

The leadership of Saudi Arabia had no interest in promoting Arab Spring democracy movements, but a strong historic interest in supporting Palestinian self-determination. Jerusalem has one of the holiest sites in the Muslim world, over which the Saudis claim a special responsibility. The Arab Peace Initiative, regularly cited as part of any likely solution, was originated by Saudi Arabia. Shortly before the UNGA convened, Prince Turki al Faisal wrote a piece for the *New York Times* warning the US against opposing the Palestinian move in stark terms: 'Saudi Arabia would no longer be able to co-operate with America in the same way it historically has. With most of the Arab world in upheaval, the "special relationship" between Saudi Arabia and the United States would increasingly be seen as toxic by the vast majority of Arabs and Muslims, who demand justice for the Palestinian people.' This resonated widely as an intervention which the US was likely to take seriously as a counter-weight to internal pressures to support Israel. As with Turkey, Saudi Arabia used words rather than action to exert regional leadership; and explicitly against Iran, as Prince Turki cast the Palestinian bid as a chance for the US to align itself with the Arab world against Tehran.

Europe

While the European Union's foreign policy representative, Catherine Ashton, took a high profile in trying to find a compromise, she was restricted by speaking on behalf of 27 countries, each with its own history, strategic interest and tactical difficulties in dealing with the PLO bid to the UN. Spain, for example, was an early supporter of the Palestinian move, while Holland's instinct was to support Israel.

The countries most likely to generate a common position were France, Germany and Britain, though each had its own approach.

The *Guardian* reported on 12 September 2011: 'In the UK, 59% of those polled said the government should vote in favour of a UN resolution recognising a Palestinian state alongside Israel. In France and Germany, the figures were 69% and 71% respectively. Support for the Palestinians' right to have their own state, without reference to the UN vote, was even higher: 71% in the UK, 82% in France and 86% in Germany.

Despite these dilemmas, there was a welcome sense among EU nations that they might at last have a role in shaping the outcome rather than merely underwriting it with development aid. And the general urge to establish an EU role in world diplomacy was a factor for France and Germany. So the European drive for compromise (which restrained the American instinct to dictate terms, gave pause to Israeli tactical thinking and bolstered Palestinian determination) was as much about projecting a perception of world influence through diplomacy as about the technicalities of the diplomacy itself.

The need to stand with Arab self-determination was both a just diplomatic end and a matter of identity – Europe on the right side of modern history – which ran into conflict with the Atlantic alliance and with Europe's post-war obligation to Israel.

The event

At the UN General Assembly, President Obama spoke first, making clear that he did not regard the UN as the route to agreement, which could come only through negotiations. He stressed Israel's security concerns and the US's 'unshakeable' support for a nation surrounded by countries who wanted to destroy it. The words themselves were standard – unshakeable, the cliché adjective of choice on this issue – but what mattered was the context not the language itself. Had President Obama been speaking to a Jewish audience on the US campaign trail or giving an interview to the Jerusalem Post, the language would have been unremarkable. But in the context of this UN meeting, they were more than words, they were a strategic act. President Obama was moving decisively away from two years of trying to mediate, into a position of identification with Israel. As significant as the words he spoke were those the President did not speak. The *Guardian* commented: 'But he offered no new initiatives and, tellingly, did not repeat earlier calls – for which he has come under fire – for negotiations to be based on the borders at the time of the 1967 war, with agreed land swaps. He also made no mention of settlements.'

This was an example of a strategic shift made by what was not said.

'He... put himself squarely as a champion of the status quo,' David Rothkopf, a visiting fellow at the Carnegie Endowment for International Peace, told the

New York Times. So the speech not only ended two years of attempted US peace-dealing on this issue, but gave an unmistakable signal about America's strategic direction in relation to the Arab and Muslim world at a time of uncharted change in the Middle East.

This important shift in US international strategy was an achievement for the Israeli government's own strategic communications campaign, waged for many months, with Prime Minister Netanyahu's Congress speech as its centrepiece. David Rothkopf said Mr Netanyahu 'has managed to read the U.S. political situation perfectly, making Obama acutely aware that he could be losing part of his base, and that, I think, in turn is what has locked Obama in'.

The point about Mr Obama's base is that several commentators were warning him that his previous, more even-handed policy was losing him support among Americans Jews, especially after a Jewish district in New York went Republican for the first time in a century a few days before the UN meeting. In fact, as noted earlier, Gallup was pointing out that the decline in President Obama's approval among Jewish voters almost exactly matched his decline among all voters. But this was a case of perception overwhelming reality. Whatever Gallup's data showed, President Obama had perceived the urgent need to give a pro-Israel speech with an impact in the real world, way beyond Brooklyn.

Meanwhile Mr Netanyahu's domestic approval

immediately rose, giving him greater confidence to set the terms of any diplomacy that followed the UN meeting. The Quartet responded to the Palestinian UN bid by issuing a call for a new attempt at negotiations which it, rather than only the US, would try to mediate. If the EU and Russia managed, through the Quartet, to end the US monopoly on the peace process, that would be a real strategic gain for the PLO.

Whether or not President Abbas achieves this strategic gain (he did not in 2012, for the Quartet's effort joined a long list of failed initiatives), he had immediately strengthened himself at home. Cheering crowds watched the live broadcast of his UN speech in town squares on the West Bank, and though this was not an entirely spontaneous outpouring of public affection, all commentators were agreed that a hitherto uninspiring leader had genuinely inspired his people. In the context of the Arab Spring, in which long-established leaderships felt vulnerable, this was worth achieving. And though it was offset by the American shift to Israel, President Abbas's supporters could argue that this was no loss, given the 20-year failure of US diplomacy to make the two-state solution anything more than diplomatic jargon. A Palestinian President battling for public support against Hamas emerged stronger in that contest for having stood up to the US President, even if Palestine was still not a free country.

So the immediate effect of the Palestinian drama at the UN was that each of the three main leaders – Abbas,

Netanyahu and Obama – appealed with some success to core domestic supporters. But there were few if any international consequences because the situation was successfully deadlocked by Israel's public diplomacy focused not on the UN but on the US Congress. There was no movement towards Palestinian independence. The UN Security Council's technical committee on applications for membership decided not to recommend in Palestine's favour, partly because the PLO could not claim full control of the territory, with Hamas in charge of Gaza. President Abbas re-invigorated his efforts to re-unite with Hamas and form a unity government, to which the Israeli government responded by withholding revenues on which the PA government was sorely dependent. Meanwhile Congress carried out its threat to halt US funding if the PLO went to the UN. The Quartet called for negotiations and asked for no 'provocations'. But Israel announced a series of decisions to accelerate settlement building, while Mr Netanyahu continued to repeat his message that he was ready for talks with no pre-conditions.

Since this is a story with no apparent end, the case study closes here, though the intense waging of the battle of strategic narratives will continue.

There are many lessons to be learned from the fascinating episode, among them that it is damaging to declare intentions without the means or the resilience to deliver. Prime Minister Netanyahu's skilled public campaign focused on Congress was possible only because

President Obama did not follow through, having said he wanted Palestine represented at the UN General Assembly. Whether or not he could or should have delivered is outside the scope of this analysis. The point here is that the President did not judge the range of possibilities as well as the Israeli Prime Minister, taking account of the mood in Congress. Public diplomacy and international strategy cannot be successful without shrewd tactical assessments made before the moment of public commitment. Wishful thinking does not make good policy. Public diplomacy fails if fine words are not followed up in practice.

This is not to say that strategists should always be timid when approaching challenges with low chances of success but high incentives to make the effort. But if bold pronouncements with high stakes are to be made, there is trouble ahead if no plan has been made for delivery, and alongside it a tactical campaign of public expectation-setting, accompanied by interventions to pressure other parties publicly. What was strikingly absent from President Obama's tactics on this issue was any effort to describe the possible disadvantages for Israel in the status quo. It must always be part of the plan to present a complex and difficult situation as a matter of choice, in which there are risks attached to others' desired outcomes. Otherwise, it is easy for others to portray your own intentions as the risk. This point is not a judgement of Israeli, Palestinian or US national interests, but an observation on technique. Most international issues are by definition a matter of choice, since there is more than one party and therefore more than one way of seeing the situation. So it is generally accurate as well as good tactics to point out the possible penalties on both sides of the equation. President Obama did not do this. He let Prime Minister Netanyahu set his agenda.

But the Israeli leader focused on only one international audience, the US Congress (that is, not US opinion overall, but one accurately identified segment with the power to achieve his objective). His strategy appeared to accept that some loss of support in other international audiences was a reasonable price. It is rare for a country to make such a calculation: most often, the aim is to achieve the greatest support as widely as possible. So in most cases, international strategy must balance the impact of a country's words and actions with different audiences, sometimes involving a conflict between strategic priorities.

Clearly the conduct of Israeli and US diplomacy around the UN meeting in September 2011 was a case where the options for international communications strategy were limited by domestic political pressures. Such pressures can be used by opponents, and international strategists must study with care the domestic pressures on others – and on themselves.

One year on, it was even clearer that the Israeli Prime Minister's public diplomacy had achieved a major tactical gain at the expense of the Palestinian President by placing tight limits on US room for manoeuvre. Mahmoud Abbas's 2012 address to the UN General Assembly was a muted lament for the two-state solution, evoking no interest on the Palestinian street. President Obama, preoccupied with more urgent Middle East concerns following the murder of the US Ambassador to Libya, was under no pressure to make more than the briefest reference to the Israel-Palestine question. Mr Netanyahu himself was free to concentrate on Iran, also barely mentioning the Palestinian question: in its way an extraordinary feat of marginalisation.

But the Israeli Prime Minister had meanwhile on Iran demonstrated the cost of unsuccessful public diplomacy. His efforts to push the US President into a commitment to use military action were a striking example of public diplomacy as a means to strategic ends. Throughout the summer of 2012, Binyamin Netanyahu used off the record media briefings and occasional on the record comments to heighten expectations that Israel would take pre-emptive military action against Iran before the US Presidential election on 6 November. President Obama used the media in response to discourage Israel. Sensing that the White House was firm against military action on Israel's timetable, Mr Netayahu switched to briefing that he wanted the US to announce a 'red line' which Iran must not cross. When Secretary of State Hillary Clinton dismissed this idea, the Israel Prime Minister responded with unusually open criticism. The US media took this badly. And polling made clear that US Jewish opinion was moving towards Barack Obama, against Mitt Romney, who had allied himself more closely with Mr Netanyahu than is general thought wise during an international tour which would by itself be a fruitful study in 'public diplomacy (how not to)'. Sensing that he was losing traction in Washington, Binyamin Netanyahu used his General Assembly address to re-set his own clock, talking of Iran passing a red line by the summer of 2013. So a grave matter of war and peace had been settled by a test of strength through the media alone, not by military muscle or diplomatic activity.

Chapter Nine

Conclusions

One common theme of these examples has been the power of words to define actions. It is often good practice to find a simple phrase to summarise complex aims, but care must be taken not to choose a phrase that will be confounded by reality. For example, Robin Cook had begun as Foreign Secretary by setting a high standard for government action with a speech that came to be known by the phrase 'ethical foreign policy'. Actually, he had talked of foreign policy needing 'an ethical dimension', which he regarded as unarguable rather than impossibly ambitious. During his subsequent media troubles the phrase 'ethical foreign policy' came to be almost a term of ridicule as 'ethical' was measured against decisions like maintaining the legal requirement, under contract, to supply spare parts for Hawk jets to an oppressive regime in Indonesia.

The 'ethical' problem was an example of a phrase that takes on an inconvenient life of its own. Robin Cook never disowned the phrase, but neither did he perpetuate it, nor seek to justify it against successful interventions with a very clear ethical dimension, like preventing the violent overthrow of the Sierra Leone government by rebels with a shocking human rights record; or indeed Kosovo.

John Major had a similar problem with his neat formula, putting Britain 'at the heart of Europe', to summarise his change of approach from Margaret Thatcher's increasingly hostile relationship with Brussels in her final phase as Prime Minister. The phrase could not bear the weight of the strengthening opinion among his backbenchers that the heart of Europe was not where Britain should be. Core phrases to summarise policy must relate to reality, or they will become serious disabilities in strategic communication.

The 'heart of Europe' did not relate to reality because the governing party had been moving for some time in the opposite direction. Margaret Thatcher's speech in Bruges in 1988 was a prime example of strategy made by words rather than deeds. Indeed it is an illustration of the power of public diplomacy to shape events, which has been the main theme of this book. I was in the audience as a reporter and it was clear that the Prime Minister thoroughly intended to make unmistakably clear a hardening of Britain's approach to Europe, not least because her press secretary Bernard Ingham had signalled this with characteristic vigour on the way there. Her core passage was: 'We have not successfully rolled back the frontiers of the state in Britain only to see them re-imposed at European level, with a European super-state exercising a new dominance from Brussels.'

This is an argument which continues to divide British politics and was still resonating when David Cameron vetoed treaty changes during the eurozone crisis in 2011. For all the changes in media and politics over more than two decades between these two Prime Ministers, the strategic calculation is similar. Both Prime Ministers identified British interests in Europe with political advantage at home, and acted with gamblers' instincts on big international gestures. Margaret Thatcher's context was that the President of the European Commission, Jacques Delors, had recently made a speech predicting 'an embryo European state within six years'. His timing was awry, but the eurozone crisis created pressures for economic integration that some would see as close to the Delors vision. The Bruges speech was made around the time that Delors and others were taking early decisions in the creation of the eurozone. As Hugo Young says in his Thatcher biography *One of Us*: 'The Bruges speech looked like a watershed in September 1988, and time has not altered that assessment.'

Looking back with the perspective of more than 20 years, it can be seen that the landscape of Britain's troubled relationship with Europe was sketched out and to an extent shaped by a single speech. Mrs Thatcher's key word 'superstate' was still resounding at Nice twelve years later, and beyond; her simple characterisation of nation versus Brussels still the core of the argument during the Blair, Brown and Cameron years, on into the British response to the eurozone crisis. The argument over this fundamental question of international strategy may possibly have taken much the same course if Mrs Thatcher had never made the Bruges speech, but her intervention shows the power of a skilled communicator to capture complexity – or over-simplify subtle situations – with the words they chose in suitably dramatic contexts. It is also worth noting the power of the media in this. It suited Margaret Thatcher's style to have a sizeable opponent, if necessary built up by the media to be big enough for her scorn. *The Sun*'s headline 'Up Yours, Delors' was seminal.

David Cameron had no single bogeyman against whom to identify himself, rather a sense of failure in the eurozone, from which his party and much of the press were urging him protect the British economy. He gladly adopted the advice of a backbencher at Prime Minister's Questions to show some bulldog spirit in Brussels. Cameron had learned hard lessons in the domestic impact of Europe when special advisor to the Chancellor on 'Black Wednesday' in 1992, when the Major government raised interest rates to punitive levels in a futile attempt to keep sterling at the level required by membership of the Euro's forerunner, the exchange rate mechanism. That government was well behind in the polls from then until its heavy defeat in 1997. Mr Cameron's 'bulldog' moment, refusing to take part in the treaty negotiations necessary for a more integrated eurozone, achieved a modest increase in his party's ratings, putting it ahead of the opposition for the first time all year in some polls. (The boost was short-lived: though the alternative might, by opening up divisions within the Coalition and within the Conservative Party, have led to a sustained fall in approval.)

The crisis in the eurozone was the most dramatic and dangerous evidence, for those countries concerned, of the growing importance of the financial markets as an audience for public diplomacy. While the threats to countries like Italy and Greece, Spain and Portugal, were fundamentally economic, there was an important element of international reputation management involved. France fought hard to maintain its international credit rating in December 2011 by a familiar device of conventional public diplomacy: attacking Britain. In Greece, George Papandreou lost office not because of an economic event, but because international patience with Greece's economic troubles snapped when he suddenly announced a referendum on austerity measures, without consulting or even informing other European leaders. They lost confidence in his will to introduce the measures on which their support depended. This was a terminal failure to match domestic pressures – the public demand to be consulted – with international sentiment. The Papandreou government needed international support more than domestic consent at a particular moment, but lost the one by striving for the other.

International sentiment is less easy to measure than

economic statistics, and though it is closely tied to hard facts like the cost of borrowing, market judgements are not entirely objective. There can be no certainty that Italy would have lost market confidence as dramatically as it did at the end of 2011, had the technocrat Prime Minister Mario Monti been installed earlier, following one of the scandals that had helped to bring ridicule on Silvio Berlusconi. The word 'technocrat' is a masterpiece of reputation management in the international political-financial market place. A rise in Italian government borrowing rates back to crisis levels did not threaten the Monti administration, despite its having no parliamentary majority nor any electoral mandate, both of which Berlusconi had maintained for longer than any Italian PM for many years. The financial markets, and fellow EU leaders, seemed content for the moment to judge the technocratic Mario Monti competent to handle the situation, as they had not his politically-damaged predecessor.

So we are entering an era in which public diplomacy presents new challenges – the financial markets, instant communications, citizen journalism by digital technology – while the traditional challenges remain. Countries as diverse in size and culture as Turkey and Tunisia, Italy and Israel, as well as the United States itself, have made recent gains or suffered setbacks through successes or failures in the way they have pursued their strategic objectives through public diplomacy. Russia's reputation has been threatened by its handling of domestic protests over allegations of election-rigging in 2011and the jail-ing of the all-girl pop group Pussy Riot in 2012, an event which dramatised a sense of growing authoritarianism under President Putin. A famous picture of Putin, stripped to the waist and carrying a gun, had domestic appeal as an image of a strong leader, but also became symbolic of a willingness to resort to strong-arm tactics. And it is impossible yet to guess whether China will at some stage have to accommodate itself to international judgement of its record on political and human rights, as it over-takes America as the world's leading economic power; or whether, on the contrary, China will be too strong to need concern itself with international reputation.

In the midst of all this change, there remains a note of optimism. Public diplomacy is becoming of greater importance because public opinion matters more. In other words, the more that governments around the world feel they must take some account of the views of their people, so it becomes more important to other countries to seek to influence those people – to inform, persuade and even to mobilise them.

Ten Core Insights

1.   Strategy Public diplomacy should be seen as a legitimate and powerful instrument for achieving a country's strategic goals, by making room for actions, changing others' perceptions and affecting their decisions.

2.   Credibility Public diplomacy must be an accurate reflection of ambiguous realities and of a country's actions. Avoid over-statement. Do not go beyond the known facts.

3.   Influence The course of events can be shaped by setting benchmarks and by making strong statements of intent which deter others.

4.   Conflict Countries need to make their vital interests clear, or risk conflict by failing to set thresholds for action.

5.   Audiences Successful public diplomacy must balance different and sometimes conflicting impacts on international audiences.

**6.	Effect** Making achievements of substance is often not enough to advance a country's international reputation and improve its situation – public diplomacy is needed to turn such achievements into gains.

**7.	Priority** Leaders must respect their duty to explain, and empower senior officials to organise coherent public diplomacy, not delegate this as a relatively unimportant task.

**8.	Negotiation** The media activity around an international negotiation can be used as a tool of diplomacy, by building relationships of respect with the media.

**9.	Language** Use simple everyday words, avoiding the jargon of diplomacy.

10. Resilience Never give up on battles that seem hopeless causes, or give in to relentless media pressure – engage.

Matthews on Modern Leadership
Robin Matthews

Leadership is not just for Generals and Chief Executives. In modern organisations, everyone needs to take responsibility and to show leadership in their own working lives. This makes leadership models that rely on exceptional figures – whether Alexander the Great or Steve Jobs – so impractical and unrealistic.

Robin Matthews takes his experience of leadership – from heading a political party to commanding the Light Dragoons in Afghanistan – and distills the timeless elements of effective leadership, such as honesty, trust, and vision. But he also shows how each individual needs to find their own way to lead, building with their own character and drawing on their personal experience and talents.

Gill on Public Policy Research
Mark Gill

We all agree that policies should be based on sound evidence of people's real needs and of what works best. But where does that evidence come from? Are focus groups a valuable tool or a dangerous distraction? How can you judge whether people are telling the whole truth when they answer opinion surveys? Or predict how people will react to new laws or taxes? And how do you go about commissioning research that is credible and affordable, and then interpret the findings?

Using examples from his own projects within the UK public service and internationally, from single employee surveys to major, intergrated research programmes, Mark Gill sets out the potential of research and the pitfalls of method, interpretation and project management. Written for policy-makers and managers, it is also an eye-opening guide for the general reader on this daunting but influential field.